Homemade

with love ♡

The Giving of oneself and one's time feels good, and in a world often said to be divided between those who spend money in order to save time and those who spend time in order to save money, our time is still seen as the ultimate luxury...

Homemade

101 Beautiful and Useful Craft Projects You Can Make at Home

Ros Badger and Elspeth Thompson

Photographs by Benjamin J. Murphy

Skyhorse Publishing

Dearest Elspeth,
Without you this book would have never been.
Thank you for all of the memories but mostly for being a
wonderful and inspiring friend.

To our mothers, Ruth and Margaret,
and our daughters, Martha, Ceidra, and Mary, who taught and continue to teach us so much

Skyhorse Publishing books may be purchased in bulk at special
discounts for sales promotion, corporate gifts, fund-raising, or
educational purposes. Special editions can also be created to
specifications. For details, contact the Special Sales Department,
Skyhorse Publishing, 555 Eighth Avenue, Suite 903, New York, NY
10018 or info@skyhorsepublishing.com.

www.skyhorsepublishing.com

10 9 8 7 6 5 4 3 2 1

Library of Congress Cataloging-in-Publication Data is available on
file.
ISBN: 978-1-61608-078-5

Printed in China

Contents

Introduction

HOMEMADE. When searching for a title for this book, there was really only one candidate in our minds: this well-worn word that conjures up both things handmade at home, and a home that's made with love.

Home, for us, is where our creativity was nurtured and continues to grow. We were both born into families who, out of necessity as much as inclination, made clothes, grew their own vegetables, and cooked from scratch rather than buying ready-made items from the shops. Ros can remember being taught to crochet, aged seven, by her grandmother, and making a doll's blanket of which she was inordinately proud. Elspeth only has to look at photographs of herself and her younger sisters in matching homemade dresses to be transported back to a happy, yet industrious, childhood where everyone seemed forever to be sewing, knitting, or making things.

There was a time, not so very long ago, when "homemade" had become synonymous with dowdiness, a degree of drudgery, and doing without. From the profligate Eighties on, shopping was the preferred national pastime, while making your own was seen as second best, if not an eccentricity, or a leftover from childhood television programs, such as *Blue Peter*.

Not so nowadays. Making things—whether sewing, cooking, or customizing clothes—is firmly in fashion, with clothes designers incorporating crochet and patchwork into their collections and celebrities as keen to be photographed with their knitting as they were with a yoga mat a few years ago. Wearing homemade clothes is something to be proud rather than ashamed of—living proof of your creativity and resourcefulness, as is sending homemade cards, or taking homemade jam, sweets, or chutney as a dinner party gift. Making your own clothes or home furnishings is also a sure-fire way to get noticed in what is becoming an increasingly homogeneous society.

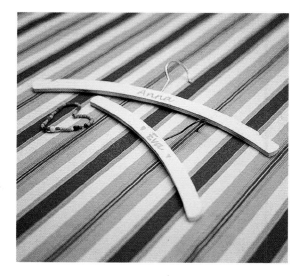

Of course, *Homemade* is not merely about style. What began as a gradual *zeitgeist* shift a few years ago—with a knitting and crochet revival, the resurgence in home-baking and general domesticity, and everyone from New York bankers to teenage schoolgirls starting crafts clubs—has gained momentum recently, aided and abetted by the environmental and financial crises that face us all.

Making and growing things not only helps save money and benefits the environment (less manufacturing means less "embodied energy" means less waste), the activities themselves give rise to a feel-good factor that can help cheer us up in adversity. Our homes become havens in times of global uncertainty, and knowing that we have the skills and resources to make things of use and beauty for those we live around and love—without costing the earth—can be a source of great comfort and pleasure. Making something for someone else with love, whether a cake for their birthday, a pair of warm woolly gloves, or a simple greeting card, can be a satisfying thing to do in itself, for children and adults alike. Giving of oneself and one's time feels good, and in a world often said to be divided between those who spend money in order to spend time and those who save time in order to save money, our time is still seen as the ultimate luxury.

The "homemade movement" is gathering momentum, with all sorts of people who may never have thought of making things becoming converts. This book is for them as much as for the more experienced, with many of the projects requiring no previous skills—and plenty of information on how to get started with knitting, crocheting, sewing, and so on. How it differs from many of the other books and articles on similar subjects is that the sentiment expressed in the subtitle is more than skin-deep. Many of the projects published elsewhere begin with a "shopping list" of stuff to buy; surely something of a contradiction in terms if the aim is to be resourceful and economical.

What we'd rather start off with is a new mindset—one that involves looking around and seeing what you have to start with, before going out to stores. Saving fabric from favorite old clothes or furnishings, buttons from worn-out clothing, and ribbon from unwrapped presents becomes second nature once you start—and as these saved and salvaged materials become stitched and woven into new objects, the backdrop to our lives gathers texture and richness, with added layers of memory and association. (We haven't quite reached the level of the old lady who claimed to have a tin in her attic labeled "pieces of string too small to be useful," but sometimes we feel we are getting there!)

You will find that you start seeing potential in everything around you. Nature remains one of our greatest resources and, for this reason, the projects in the book are arranged around the seasons. As the saying goes, if life offers you lemons, make lemonade—and the changing months offer both new materials to use and colors and textures to be inspired by, as illustrated in the photographs of nature that appear throughout the book.

We hope that this approach will encourage you to try a few of the projects listed, maybe even adding to or adapting them according to your own ideas, inclinations, and aspirations. Whatever you make, we hope you enjoy the process—and the feeling of pride and satisfaction that are part and parcel of the result. Most of all, we hope you will be able to take pleasure in saying, when asked where you bought or found the cake, dress, or cushion in question: "It's homemade. I made it myself."

We haven't quite reached the level of the old lady who claimed to have a tin in her attic labeled "pieces of string too small to be useful," but sometimes we feel we are getting there!

spring

Valentine's Day
ideas

SIDESTEP THE CRASS COMMERCIALIZATION of Valentine's Day with simple handmade gifts or tokens that mean so much more than store-bought flowers or cards. The ideas shown on these pages are not at all difficult to make— indeed, some take only minutes—but are still lovely objects to treasure and keep. Paint a poem on paper, customize vintage cards, or make a paper cut-out by folding the paper concertina-style, marking a design in pencil and snipping out with sharp scissors. Write a message on a heart-shaped pebble, fashion a twiggy heart from whippy branches, or thread beads or buttons on to wire and bend into shape. Sometimes the simplest ideas are the most effective— surprise your partner with a heart formed from the family's shoes on the floor to greet them when they come downstairs in the morning, or write a quirky message in pebbles or leaves on the lawn.

♥ Thread buttons on to thick wire, bend into shape, and secure with a knot behind one of the buttons—pretty beads or sequins would work just as well.

Paint or chalk a message on a heart-shaped pebble—finding the pebble is the hard part!

♥ Stitch together some scraps of fabric with romantic associations—from some favorite old shirts, for instance—and cut out two heart shapes. With right sides facing, sew together, leaving a small gap for turning through. Turn right sides out and use fancy traditional stitches to decorate the seams. Then stuff with dried lavender (see page 62) and stitch the gap to close.

Using pinking shears, cut out two heart shapes from contrasting colors of felt, one piece slightly smaller than the other. Embroider a simple message on the smaller one, and perhaps a few flowers, and attach to the other by sewing neatly around the edges. Add stick-on beads or sequins (if not using flowers) and a ribbon loop for hanging.

Egg
cosies

THESE COLORFUL EGG COSIES and overleaf will always cheer up your breakfast table as well as keeping your boiled eggs warm. Simple enough for quite small children to make under adult supervision, they also make great Easter presents, maybe decorated with the recipient's name and sitting on a nest of chocolate or marzipan eggs. Small items such as this are good ways of using up odd pieces of felt and thread, which might otherwise be wasted. And yet an egg cosy can definitely be defined as a luxury: a non-essential item that nevertheless enhances the enjoyment of one of life's simple pleasures.

You will need
◆ Pieces of felt and leftover scraps in different colors
◆ Sewing thread in various colors to contrast with the felt

To make the chicken cosy (opposite)
♥ Using the chicken pattern on page 236, cut out two pieces for the body and, in a contrasting color, two pieces for the wings. Pin a wing to each chicken shape and sew the rounded end of the wings to the chicken's body using over stitch (see page 226).

♥ Make the eyes by stitching a star shape on each chicken piece in the middle of the head. Alternatively, sew a button on either side.

♥ Place the chicken pieces wrong sides together and pin to hold. Then sew around the chickens from the bottom right-hand corner to the bottom left-hand corner with blanket stitch, or running stitch if preferred (see pages 225–6). In a different color, work blanket stitch along the bottom edge.

To make the simple cosy (page 23)
♥ Using the simple egg cosy pattern on page 236, cut out three pieces of felt in contrasting colors.

♥ Using scrap pieces of felt, decorate each piece with a motif of your choice. We cut out a flower for one of the cosies (you might choose to use the pattern on page 236) and letters for another (for example, "EGG," "DAD," "MOM"). Sew on the motifs on with running stitch.

♥ Pin together two pieces of the cosy with wrong sides facing and sew along the seam with over stitch in a contrasting color of thread. Add the third piece and sew along the two remaining seams with over stitch.

These colorful egg cosies will always cheer up your breakfast table.

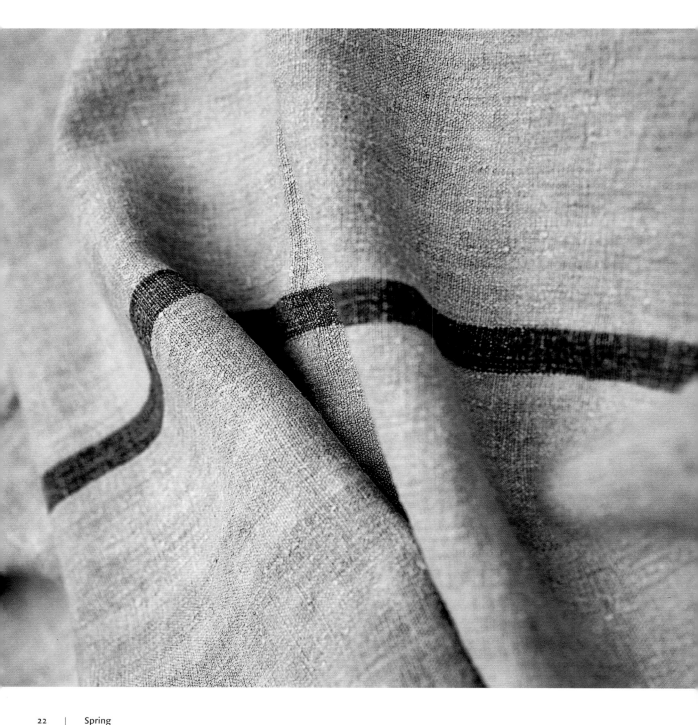

Pin the egg on the
chicken

THIS DELIGHTFUL PAINTED BANNER can be brought out every year for Easter parties or spring birthdays. Not only does it look decorative, it also provides the basis for good old-fashioned fun in the form of the traditional blindfold game—a variation on Pin the Tail on the Donkey.

You will need

◆ A plain cotton or linen sheet
◆ Washable paints or inks
◆ Assortment of paintbrushes
◆ Stiff paper or card
◆ Scotch tape
◆ A blindfold

To make and play

♥ Using the sheet as the canvas, apply your design with the washable paints or inks. See the tips on page 28 for copying and transferring pictures or designs on to fabric, or ask a talented friend or child to draw the pictures by hand.

♥ While the banner is drying, draw ten or so egg shapes on to the paper or card, decorate in an assortment of egg colors and cut out when dry. Just before you play the game, add a loop of Scotch tape to the back of each egg for attaching it to the banner. This is much safer for children than using pins.

♥ To play the game, hang the banner against a wall or from the branches of a low-growing tree— we pegged ours to a clothes line (see overleaf). Blindfold each player by turn, spin them around slowly twice, pencil their name on the back of an egg, and ask them to attach it to the picture as near to where the chicken would have laid it as they can. When everyone has had a go, the winner is the one whose egg is nearest to the right place.

Variations

Make a series of seasonal banners for party fun throughout the year: pin the nose (or broom) on the witch for Halloween; the horns on the reindeer for Christmas; the wand on the fairy or the cherry on the cake for all-purpose birthdays, and so on. The possibilities are endless!

Tips on handpainting

Several of the projects in this book were handpainted by Mary Mathieson (as well as the Easter banner on the previous page, see also the Lavender cats on page 62 and the Advent calendar on page 202). If you are not particularly artistic yourself, it may be worth commissioning a clever friend or acquaintance to help with some of the ideas, particularly if, like the banner and calendar, they have the potential to become family heirlooms. But it is important not to be too precious about these things. Children's drawings have a wonderful spontaneity about them, which it would be fun to preserve. Simple potato prints and/or abstract freehand patterns can look great if you choose the right colors. And your own freehand attempts may surprise you, if you are bold enough to try.

♥ Try copying an existing design, using graph paper and tracing paper. The Internet is a fabulous instant source of all kinds of patterns and images that can be copied or customized. Just click on to Google Images and search for the type of picture or pattern you want. You can also search for fonts for letters, as used for the Painted hangers on page 41. Print out the design, scale it up using graph paper (if necessary) and then transpose, using tracing paper and pencil, to the place where it is needed.

♥ Use fabric paints or fabric crayons to color in and define your design. These come in many colors, including metallic shades. Don't be afraid to make sweeping strokes and be creative— freehand drawing buzzes with creative energy.

♥ Before making your decorated fabric into banners, clothes, or soft furnishings, fix the fabric paint or crayon designs in place by ironing them as the instructions specify. Your design should then be machine washable.

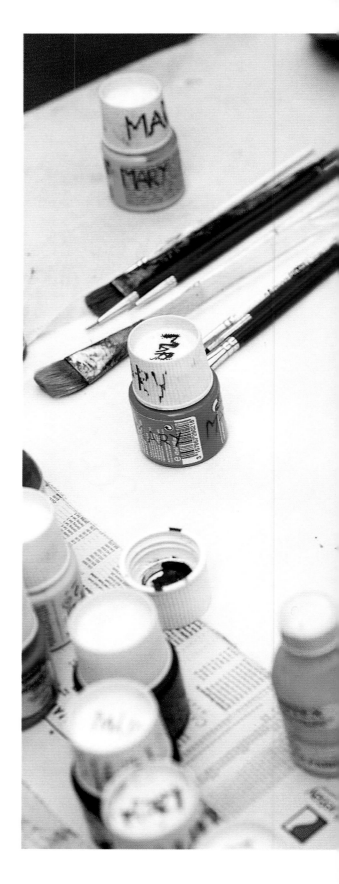

Natural
cleaning materials

ONCE YOU'VE GOT into the *Homemade* mindset, you may find that mixing your own cleaning materials from natural ingredients makes more sense than using specific cleaning products. Why spend money filling your cupboards with garishly packaged potions and powders, often brimming with chemicals that can cause allergies and other health problems, when these natural, cheap, and readily available solutions work just as well, if not better—and often smell sweeter, to boot? Here are just a few we have found effective.

DRAINS: Once a month, pour a kettle full of boiling water over a cup or two of soda crystals in order to keep your drains free and fragrant.

FINGER MARKS ON WALLS AND PAINTWORK: Rub with a chunk of fresh white bread.

GROUTING ON TILES: Scrub with a toothbrush, using a paste made from baking soda and lemon juice.

LIMESCALE IN KETTLES: Fill with distilled white vinegar and leave overnight. Rinse well afterwards.

LIMESCALE ON TAPS: Rub with a paste of distilled white vinegar and baking soda. Or soak a paper towel in fresh lemon juice, wrap around the tap, cover with a plastic bag, and leave overnight. Wipe clean.

MILDEW: Wipe with distilled white vinegar.

POTS AND PANS: Add to half a cup of soap flakes mixed with enough water to fill the pan. When cold, wash.

REFRIGERATOR: Wipe all the surfaces inside with a paste of one tablespoon of baking soda in a little hot water (also dispels odors).

SMELLY PET BEDDING OR ODOROUS SHOES: Sprinkle with baking soda overnight and shake or brush out the next day.

STAINED TEA AND COFFEE CUPS: Brush with a paste of baking soda and a little water.

STUBBORN STAINS ON BATH AND/OR TUBE SINKS: Wipe with a paste of baking soda and water or cream of tartar and lemon juice.

TILED FLOORS: Wash with a mix made from equal quantities of water and distilled white vinegar.

UNIVERSAL FABRIC STAIN REMOVER: Dab the stained fabric with fresh lemon juice and leave in bright sunlight, or (for more sensitive colors and fabrics) rub with soda crystals before hand washing.

WINDOWS: Wipe with distilled white vinegar and rub dry with newspaper. For very dirty panes, sponge with eco-friendly dish soap first.

Easter
tree

HANGING HAND-DECORATED EGGS on branches of spring leaves and blossom is a lovely tradition that can become part of family life. Those in the picture are a mixture of hand-painted and decorated eggshells, some of which date back 20 years or more, treasures given by friends or family or brought back from trips abroad. If you make and buy a few more eggs each year, you will soon have an heirloom collection that can be handed down to the next generation.

You will need
- Raw eggs
- Empty egg box
- Darning needle
- Bowl
- Vinegar
- Paints, felt pens, pastels, glue, paper and fabric scraps— whatever comes to hand for decorating
- Food coloring and/or onion skins (optional)
- Ribbon or fine cord with beads
- Small branches for the "tree"

To make

♥ To blow a raw egg, place it upright in the egg box and use a darning needle to make a small hole in the top. Turn the egg carefully upside down and make a slightly larger hole in the bottom. Break up the yolk by poking the needle about inside, and then gently, but steadily, blow into the smaller hole to evacuate the innards into a bowl (save for making scrambled eggs or pancakes).

♥ Rinse the egg by by submerging the shell in water with a little vinegar added and blowing out again. Allow to dry.

♥ Decorating ideas include painting with poster paints, felt pens, or pastels— anything from free-form flowers, chicks, and rabbits to polka dots, stripes, spirals, or designs that run around the circumference of the shell. Or stick on paper, fabric, pressed or imitation flowers, or other shapes— adding ribbons, bows, or other ornamentation as the fancy takes you.

♥ Most eggs have brown shells these days, but how about using blue for a change? Or, to dye white eggshells, add a few drops of food coloring (or create a natural dye such as from onion skins for a rich ochre yellow) to a pan of water with the eggshells and simmer for 10 minutes.

♥ To attach the eggs to the tree, cut a length of ribbon and glue it carefully right around the egg lengthwise, tying the free ends into a bow at the top. Alternatively, thread one end of a fine cord or ribbon through the darning needle and tie a knot in the other end. Thread a small bead on to the cord or ribbon and pass the needle through the large hole at the base of the egg and out through the smaller hole at the top. The bead should then anchor the cord or ribbon in place, allowing you to make a loop for tying at the top of the egg.

♥ After Easter, store the eggs in the empty egg box in a safe place until next year.

...a lovely tradition that can become part of family life...

Decorated
coat hangers

DECORATED COAT HANGERS not only look good in your closet, but they are practical, too, as the texture of the knitted and crocheted covers stop silky clothes from slipping off. They also make a lovely present, particularly if they are personalized with the recipient's name or some other detail. A hand-covered or painted hanger can also add that extra, personal touch when giving home-sewn, hand-me-down, or vintage clothes. You might be forgiven for thinking that the examples pictured here are time-consuming to make, but they are surprisingly quick and easy. The hanger used is a standard wooden one, 45 cm (18 in) long and 2 cm (3/4 in) wide, but you could make a shorter cover to fit a standard child's hanger, which is 32 cm (12½ in) long.

Knitted cover with optional crochet flower

The knitted cover pictured opposite is so simple that anyone able to cast on and off and do basic garter stitch could make it. There is no purl stitch, no shaping— just a simple strip like a doll's scarf. It is a great way to use up odd scraps of wool—the method below specifies 4-ply, but any weight of wool will do. Cast on stitches the width of the hanger front and back, and knit in garter stitch until the length of the hanger has been reached.

You will need

- ◆ 2 oz ball 4-ply mercerized cotton (or matt cotton) for main color (MC)
- ◆ Ends of 4-ply mercerized cotton (or matt cotton) in contrast color for crotchet flower (optional)
- ◆ Size 2 knitting needles
- ◆ 2-mm crochet hook
- ◆ Wooden coat hanger
- ◆ Darning needle
- ◆ PVA glue (optional)

Tension over garter stitch

26 sts and 48 rows = 4 in

Abbreviations

See pages 229 and 231

Measurements

18 in on top curve of coat hanger

To make the hanger cover

♥ US size 2 needles and MC, cast on 17 sts.
Work in garter st (knit every row) until strip measures length of coat hanger when slightly stretched.
Cast off.
Find the center of work in both length and width and slip over hanger hook.
Stitch the strip together on the underside of the hanger with a neat catch st. Sew both ends to close.

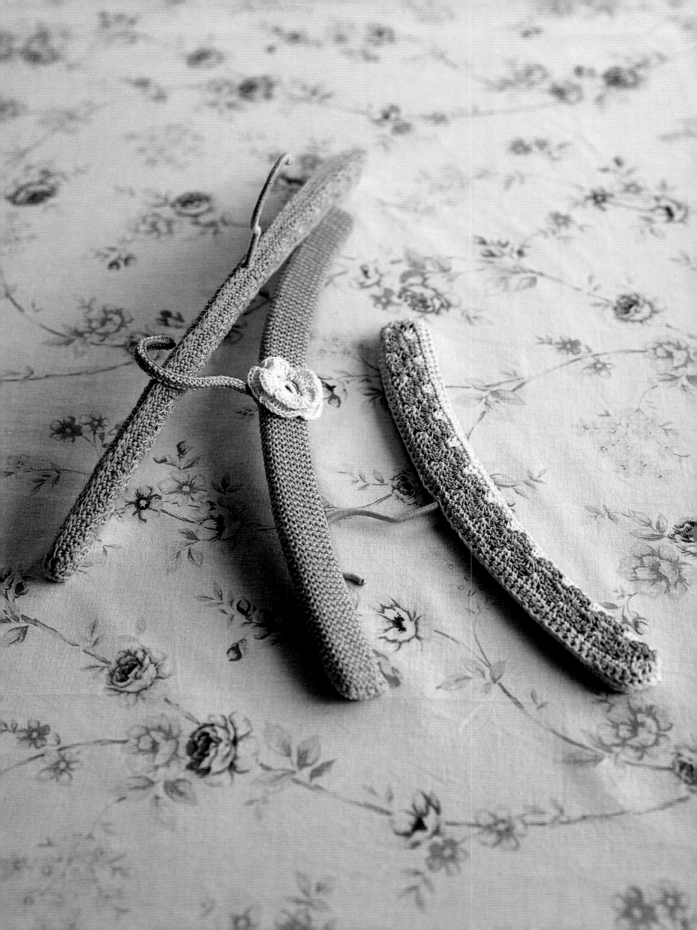

To cover a standard 5¼ in hook (optional)

♥ With US size 2 needles and MC, cast on 38 sts (measure your hanger hook and adjust accordingly).

Work 4 rows in garter st.

Cast off.

Fold around hook and sew edges together so the hook is covered.

Catch to hanger cover to avoid hook cover slipping off. Alternatively, wrap the hook with the yarn, securing at each end with a blob of PVA glue.

To make the crochet flower (optional)

♥ With 2-mm crochet hook and contrast color, make 6ch and join with a sl st.

Row 1: Work 15dc into the circle, join with a sl st.
Row 2: 1ch, 1dc in first dc,* 3ch, 1dc into 3rd dc, repeat from *. End with 3ch then sl st to first dc.

Row 3: 1ch, work a petal of (1dc, 3ch, 5tr, 3ch, 1dc) into each of next five 3ch arches, sl st to 1st dc.
Row 4: 1ch, (1dc between 2dc, 5ch behind petal of third round) five times, sl st to first dc.
Row 5: 1ch, work a petal of (1dc, 3ch, 7tr, 3ch, 1dc) into each of the five 5ch arches, sl st to first dc.
Sew flower to center of hanger.

Crocheted cover

If you are able to crochet, this cover is very pretty, using two colors of yarn in a textured pattern. If making it to go with a gift of clothes, choose colors to coordinate with them. Treasured clothes from your children's early childhood can also be hung on these hangers from the walls of their bedrooms (like the Child's summer dresses on page 72).

You will need

♦ 1 oz 4-ply cotton or wool in contrasting colors
♦ 2.25-mm crochet hook
♦ Wooden coat hanger
♦ PVA glue

Abbreviations

See page 231

Measurements

18 in on top curve of coat hanger or 12½ in child's coat hanger

To make 2

♥ The shell pattern is made up of a multiple of 6ch plus 3 turning chain. So reduce or add by six, depending on the length of your coat hanger.

This pattern is worked as 4 rows either side of the central 100 (76) chain with rows 5 and 6 worked all around the work.

♥ With 2.25-mm crochet hook and 4-ply yarn, make 100 (76) ch.

ROW 1: Work 2tr in fourth chain from hook, * miss 2ch, 1dc in next ch, miss 2ch, 5tr in next ch. Repeat from * to end, finishing with 1dc in last chain.

ROW 2: NB this row is worked along the base of chain. Sl st into side of first dc from row 1, then work 3ch, 2tr into first ch (where last dc from row 1 was made), * miss 2ch, 1dc (into chain where last group of 5tr were made on the previous row), miss 2ch, 5tr into next ch. Repeat from * to end, finishing with 1dc at end.

ROW 3: Change color, 3ch, 2tr on top of last dc from row 2, * 1dc either side of the center treble of the 5tr cluster from row 2, 3tr in next dc. Repeat from * to end.

ROW 4: Sl st down side of work and repeat row 3 above row 1.

ROWS 5 & 6: Dc all around the edge of work. Fasten off.

TO JOIN: Place two pieces together, wrong sides facing. Sl st together along bottom edge and half of top. Then place on to hanger and finish sl stitching together on to the hanger. Leave the hook bare or bind it using a length of the yarn, securing at each end with a blob of PVA glue.

Painted hangers

For tips on choosing typefaces and tracing and transferring images from your computer, see page 28.

♥ To ensure a good finish, use a couple of coats of gloss paint in your chosen color, and allow to dry completely before adding your design or name in a contrasting color.

♥ Use as little paint as is needed to create an even coverage and flat finish. It will also keep drips to a minimum. When applying the background color, paint the entire hanger and hang it on a clothesline (or similar) to dry, with newspaper beneath to catch any drips.

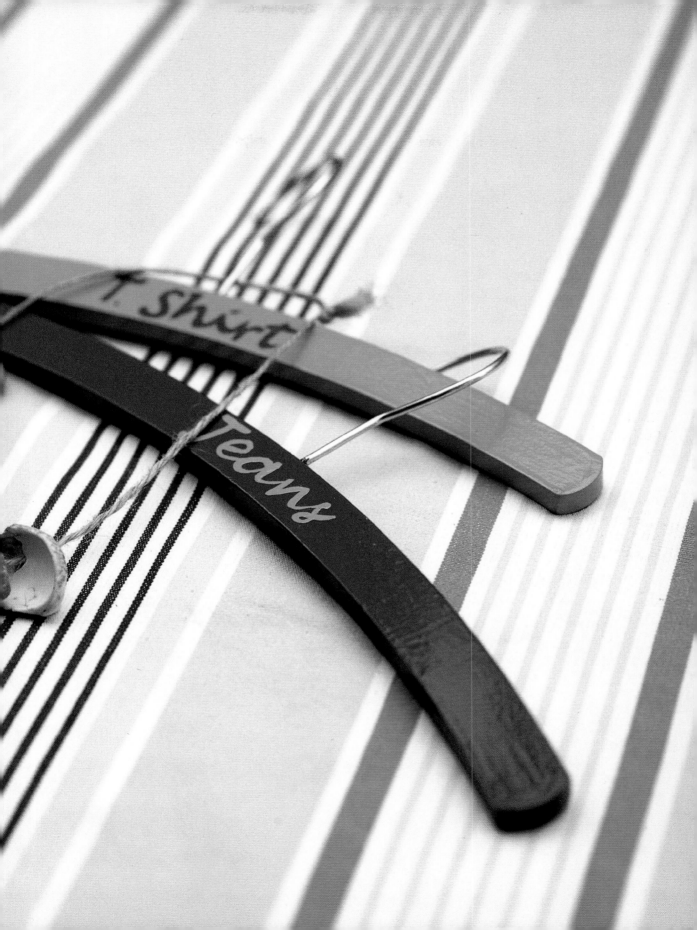

Patchwork
wall

WE LOVE PATCHWORK, both for its simple graphic patterns and the mêlée of memories and associations it can evoke. Projects such as covering a wall with scraps of paper, as here, give patchwork a modern spin, while losing none of its timeless charm and appeal. Choose just one wall in a room—alcoves or chimneys work well—or it will look overwhelming, though you might get away with it in a small downstairs bathroom. Gather lots of scraps of wallpaper. Old sample books are a great source if you can get hold of any from wallpaper shops or suppliers; otherwise raid your attic and homes of friends for leftover rolls to cut up. Like traditional fabric patchwork, this idea has far more resonance if patterns with sentimental value—the paper from your childhood bedroom or first married home, for example—are included in the mix.

You will need

- Wallpaper scraps or samples
- Plumb line
- Spirit level
- Wallpaper paste and brush
- Water and sponge
- Stepladder

To make

♥ Decide on a rough color scheme and plan how you will cover the space, distributing strong colors, patterns, and different sizes throughout. How precisely you work is a matter of personal style and temperament— perfectionists will do a trial run with Blu-tac and use a plumb line to ensure all the verticals are straight, while others will be happy to stick as they go.

♥ Paste small patches of pattern at a time, butting the edges neatly against one another and cutting pieces to fit wherever necessary. Keep checking progress by standing back to assess the effect, and when finished, sit back or lie down and drift into each pattern in turn.

Variations

Other possibilities for this treatment include postcards, cartoons, book jackets (an example of this seen in a bookshop in New York), sheet music, or maps.

Sowing
seeds

RAISING PLANTS FROM SEED is a satisfying pastime—and it saves money, too. A packet of lettuce or spinach seeds doesn't cost very much and, if sown in small batches at two-week intervals, will keep you in salad leaves all summer—just look at the price of lettuce in supermarkets and you will see what a saving this is. Your own produce can also be grown organically, without the use of artificial feeds or pesticides, and harvested at the peak of freshness. Ornamental plants for the garden border or containers can also be started off in this way. Choose annuals like sunflowers and cosmos, which germinate fast and don't need the extra heat of a greenhouse.

Starting seeds off in pots or trays is often useful, as it means the seedlings are easily identified from the "weedlings" that might spring up in open ground, and the young plants can be protected from slugs and snails until they are larger and stronger. Smaller seeds, for such plants as lettuce or violas, are best sown in trays and transplanted, or "pricked out," into pots when the first "true" leaves have formed, handling gently by the first leaves, not the delicate stems.

Avoid using plastic pots and trays, which cost energy to produce, are non-biodegradable, and are only just becoming recyclable. Instead, try to use longer-lasting wooden trays, such as those pictured overleaf (which can be personally printed), and for pots, look for salvaged terracotta, biodegradable coir, or DIY versions made from newspapers (see page 48). Always label your sowings. Recycled popsicle sticks or wooden stirrers for hot drinks are attractive and reusable.

You will need

◆ Seed tray(s) or 3-in pots
◆ Potting soil
◆ Sheet of glass or plastic, or small plastic bags (for pots)
◆ Newspaper
◆ Trowel

To sow in trays

💙 Fill the tray to the top with potting soil (ordinary dirt is too rich in nutrients), level off, and soak with water using a watering can with a medium rose head. Sprinkle the seed sparingly over the surface of the soil and cover with a fine layer of soil.

💙 Place a sheet of glass (or a plastic cover) and newspaper on top and do not water again. Check every 24 hours— some seeds germinate in a matter of days— and remove the glass and newspaper when the seedlings are up. Prick out the healthiest plants into small pots when the second set of leaves have formed.

To sow in pots

💙 Larger seeds, such as sunflowers, courgettes, or lima beans, can be sown two or three to a 7.5-cm (3-in) pot. Fill the pots with potting soil to the top and water well. Then, push one seed at a time down into the soil at the recommended depth and cover with soil.

💙 Cover with glass, or a plastic bag secured with an rubber band, to speed up germination. If the seeds all germinate, select the strongest one or two for planting out.

💙 Once the seedlings are established, keep well watered using a watering can with a fine rose head. Plant out in open ground when the roots are just beginning to emerge through the drainage holes and any danger of frost has passed.

Planting into soil or large containers

💙 Well before your seedlings are large enough to be planted, clear the ground they are to go into of weeds, giving it one last hoe or weed before the young plants go in. If the soil needs improving, work in some well-rotted compost or manure, or fork in a handful of organic fertilizer, such as seaweed or blood, fish and bone, per square foot.

💙 To plant, dig a hole at least three times the size of the rootball and water it well. Knock the plant gently out of its pot and place in the hole, filling loosely with compost and soil, so the soil levels for the plant and ground are equal. You can plant newspaper (see overleaf) and coir pots straight in the ground. Keep the plants well watered in hot, dry spells.

💙 If growing vegetables, harvest for cooking as required, trimming the plant regularly and removing at least some of the flowers to ensure plenty of fresh new growth. Remember, too, that you can collect your own seed for sowing next year.

Newspaper pots

You can buy kits to make newspaper pots— those that make more than one at a time are obviously less laborious. They all entail tearing old newspapers into strips and coiling them up to make containers to fill with dirt for sowing.

The individual wooden "pot makers" can easily be emulated by using a length of broomstick, wrapping a double thickness of newspaper about 20 cm (8 in) long around it and over the rounded end and slipping carefully off, scrunching up one end for the base of the pot. Placing the paper pots in old egg cartons helps keep them from unraveling or falling apart when watered. The joy is that the pots can be planted straight into open ground, when the time comes, without disturbing the plants' roots.

Recycled popsicle sticks make attractive, reusable labels.

Easter
garden basket

FLORISTS' SHOPS and garden centers are full of pretty spring bulbs in pots at this time of year, so pick your favorites and make an impromptu Easter garden in a traditional basket. This would make a great centerpiece for the Easter lunch table, or could be given as a present. For a lovely naturalistic look, we chose plants that might be found in a country meadow—primroses, snakeshead fritillaries (*Fritillaria meleagris*), and dwarf daffodils (2–3 of each for a medium basket, with self-seeding purple-leafed violets dug up from the garden as an edging). Once the flowers are over, the plants can be set out in the garden (or in a large pot) for next year, and the basket put to another use.

You will need

◆ A traditional wooden trug or basket
◆ Outdoor eggshell paint (see Directory, page 242)
◆ Paintbrush
◆ Black trash bag
◆ General-purpose potting soil
◆ Assortment of potted spring-flowering bulbs or other flowers in bud

To make

♥ If using a basket, give it a couple of coats of eggshell paint and leave to dry.

♥ Line the inside of the basket with plastic, cutting so that it comes just below the rim. Use a knife to make two or three slits in the base of the plastic for drainage, and anchor it in position with a handful of soil.

♥ Experiment with positioning your plants (still in pots) inside the basket until you have an attractive arrangement—tallest plants in the center, descending in height to groundcover varieties around the edges usually works best.

♥ Knock the plants gently out of their pots. Depending on the height of the soil in the pots, either add a layer of soil to the base of the basket first, or start positioning your plants, working from the center outwards.

♥ Fill in any gaps between the plants with extra soil, or with smaller plug plants or little violet or viola seedlings.

♥ Press down gently around the plants with your fingers and water well. Keep the soil moist but not sodden while the plants are in flower— they will dry out more quickly if they are kept indoors.

Thyme
carpet in a crate

BUZZING WITH BEES and studded with fragrant flowers in summer, a carpet of different thyme plants is a lovely idea. If you don't have room in your garden to plant one, don't despair! This potted version uses an old wooden box or crate instead of a sunny bank—a shallow basket would work equally well as thyme is shallow-rooted, needing only 4 in or so of soil. Choose a variety of different types of thyme with contrasting leaf sizes, scents, and colors for an attractive—and aromatic—effect. There are lemon-scented and gold- and silver-leaved species, as well as the more common broad-leaved and small-leaved types (see Directory, pages 247–9). Harvest the leaves to bring flavor to salads and cooked dishes.

You will need
- ◆ Various thyme plants to cover surface of soil
- ◆ Wooden crate, box, or basket
- ◆ Black trash bag
- ◆ Gravel, bricks, or polystyrene chips
- ◆ All-purpose soil

To make
♥ Water your plants well before planting. Place them in their pots in a large pot or tray of water for a good soaking while you prepare the container.

♥ Line the inside of the box or basket with plastic, cutting so that it comes just below the rim. Use a knife to make two or three slits in the base of the plastic for drainage. Place gravel, bricks, or polystyrene chips in the base of the container to improve the drainage and save on soil, leaving space for 4–6 in of soil at the top.

♥ Add enough soil at the bottom so that the remainder of soil in the pots is level with the top of the container (it will settle to a lower level later). Plan your arrangement with the plants still in their pots, then knock them gently out, tease out the roots a little, and plant in position. Fill in with soil between the plants and water thoroughly.

♥ Place in a sunny spot and keep well watered for the first few weeks. Harvest for cooking as required.

Harvest the leaves to bring flavor to salads and cooked dishes...

Elderflower
cordial

WITH ITS FRESH, flowery taste and fragrant aroma, elderflower cordial seems to distil the very essence of spring and early summer into a bottle. It is also incredibly easy to make. For the best flavor, gather your flowers on a warm sunny morning, and pick only those whose flowerheads are fully open and still dusty with floury yellowish pollen. Decanted into pretty bottles, with handwritten labels, this would make the perfect gift for bringing to a dinner party or weekend away. It is also lovely as a base for champagne cocktails, a sauce over ice cream, or added to a gooseberry fool to enhance its flavor. It keeps in the fridge for several weeks—if you can resist it for that long—or can be frozen in plastic bags or bottles. Some recipes require boiling but this one doesn't and so retains the true flavor of the elderflowers.

You will need

◆ 10 large heads of elderflowers (see above for when to pick them)
◆ 3 cups boiling water
◆ 1½ lb unrefined granulated sugar or a mixture of granulated sugar and muscovado
◆ 3-4 lemons, strips of zest removed and the fruit sliced
◆ Sterlized bottles (see page 233)

To make

♥ Place the elderflowers in a large stainless steel pan or plastic bucket, pour over the boiling water, add the sugar, and stir. Add the lemon slices, squeezing as you do so to release their juice, and stir in the zest.

♥ Cover with a clean damp cloth and leave somewhere cool and dark to steep for 48 hours. Strain through a sieve lined with muslin and decant into the sterilized bottles.

Variations

♥ 1 oz of citric/tartaric acid instead of lemons. This may enhance the keeping potential of the cordial, although fresh lemons give the best flavor.

♥ If you are unable to find elderflowers, fruit cordials can be made by pouring 18 fl oz of boiling water over 1 lb of fresh fruit, such as strawberries, raspberries, or blackcurrants. Then add 2 lb of granulated sugar, one zested and sliced lemon, and 1½ oz of citric/tartaric acid. Cover and leave somewhere cool and dark for 48 hours before decanting as above.

Simnel cake

WITH THEIR 11 BALLS of marzipan representing the Apostles (minus Judas, who betrayed Jesus), simnel cakes are traditional Easter fare. This recipe is a lighter version of Christmas cake, with the marzipan incorporated into the cake as well as covering it in the traditional way. Leave plain for a wholesome, minimalist look, or add a central "nest" made from cornflakes mixed with butter, cocoa, and a little light corn syrup, filled (and refilled) with foil- or sugar-coated eggs.

You will need

- 1 cup butter, softened
- 1 cup soft brown sugar
- 3 eggs
- 3 tbsp milk
- 1½ cups self-rising flour, sifted
- 1½ cups mixed dried fruit
- ½ cup mixed dried peel
- ½ cup natural glacé cherries
- 1 tsp mixed spice
- 1 tbsp black treacle
- At least 1½ cups natural marzipan
- Apricot jam, for securing marzipan
- 1 egg, beaten, for glazing

To make

Preheat the oven to 300°F. Grease and line an 8-in diameter spring-form baking pan with parchment paper.

Put the butter and sugar in a bowl and, using a hand-held electric whisk, cream together until light and fluffy. Add the eggs and milk and continue to beat together. Add the remaining ingredients, except the marzipan, and stir well. Smooth half the mixture into the base of the baking pan.

Divide the marzipan into three equal parts. Form one piece into a ball and roll out to make an 8-in round. Place on top of the mixture in the baking pan before adding the rest of the mixture.

Bake on the bottom shelf of the oven for 1 hour. Then turn down the temperature to 275°F and cook for another hour or until the top is brown, firm, and just springy to the touch. Take care not to overcook the cake— it is best if the middle is still a little soft and spongy; test by inserting a skewer into the center. Remove the cake from the oven and leave to cool.

In a small bowl, dilute 3 tablespoons of the jam with 1 tablespoon of hot water. Roll out another marzipan disc to fit the top of the cake, and use a little diluted jam to secure it in place. Make 11 balls from the remaining marzipan and position at regular intervals (again secured with a little diluted jam) around the top of the cake.

Preheat the broiler to medium. Brush the marzipan lightly with egg and glaze under the broiler for 1–2 minutes until slightly browned, taking care not to burn the marzipan. Wrap the cake in foil to store until needed (it will last for several weeks), and decorate further as you wish.

summer

Lavender
cats

LAVENDER BAGS have a somewhat quaint, old-fashioned image, but there is no reason why they cannot be updated. These hand-painted lavender cats were made as presents for Ros's daughters by our friend the artist Mary Mathieson (see Directory, page 251). They can be made in any size—tiny ones for tucking into drawers to keep clothes fresh and protect against moths, or large enough to double up as fragrant cushions. Adding dried beans to the lavender mix for the larger cats not only makes it go further but adds some welcome weight to the cushions. They make wonderful presents—and can be personalized with a name.

You will need

- Dried lavender or lavender bush for drying at home
- Plain cotton fabric (an old sheet is fine)
- Fabric paints and crayons
- Paintbrushes
- Cotton thread for machine or hand sewing

To make

♥ If you have lavender in your garden, you can dry your own flowers. Harvesting just as the top florets are opening ensures the strongest scent, but after flowering, when the blooms are already drying on the stems, is also fine. Cut the flowers with long stems and tie with string in bunches of 30 or so stems. Place the head of each bunch in a brown paper bag, tie up with string, and hang, flowers downwards, in a dry place for ten days to two weeks. When the flowers are fully dry, open the bags and pull off any remaining florets that have not fallen from the stems.

♥ To make the fabric cat bag, transfer the cat pattern on page 237 on to a piece of cotton fabric folded into two. Cut around the design, leaving ½ in all around as a seam allowance. Paint the pieces with fabric paints or crayons (see page 28 for handpainting tips). Iron to fix the design as on the following product instructions.

♥ Turn right sides together and machine or hand sew around the outline, leaving a gap of about 2 in along the bottom edge for stuffing. Snip in towards the seam on the curved edges so the bag lies flat when opened out.

♥ Turn right sides out and iron into shape, using the pointed ends of scissors to push out any awkward corners. Stuff with dried lavender—or lavender mixed with small dried beans (such as mung)—and neatly hand sew up the opening. Make sure not to get the lavender cat wet, especially if beans have been included.

Variations

If you don' t feel confident about making a cat, why not make a simple square or heart shape and decorate with abstract patterns or even potato prints? Remember that you can decorate the back, too.

Modern
patchwork

FOR CENTURIES, making patchwork has provided an attractive, economical, and absorbing way to turn scraps of old fabric into objects of real beauty. Traditionally, patchworking was made in poorer areas, as witnessed by the "kantha" cloths of India, hand-quilted from strips of old patterned saris; the patched "Boro" overalls of Japanese cotton workers, in which the original garment is scarcely identifiable beneath the patches; and the traditional American quilts of the Midwest with their descriptive names—"Log Cabin," "Tumbling Dice," and "Grandmother's Flower Garden." Love, memories, and companionship, as well as thrift, went into these pieces, which were often made in groups or quilting circles, and were handed down through generations of women. Ironically, with the passing of time, many of these once humble items are now hugely valuable, commanding high prices in antique shops and auction rooms.

Patchwork is certainly fashionable again, with many people trying their hand at making their own, as well as collecting old examples. Some are drawn to the old patterns and techniques, using templates and intricate hand sewing. But patchwork can be given a modern spin, the homespun aesthetic partnered with sharp contemporary tailoring, as in designs by Paul Smith and Vivienne Westwood, or with sleek modern furniture, such as the silk patchwork cushions on classic white plastic Saarinen chairs, seen in the window of the Designer's Guild shop. We even spotted an amazing patchwork sofa by Squint (see Directory, page 251). (See also the Patchwork wall featured on page 42.)

Such ambitious projects may be somewhere down the line, unless you are already a patchwork aficionado, but there's no reason why patchwork has to be fussy and fiddly. Start saving pieces of fabric now—from favorite outgrown children's clothes, shirts that have worn at the collars and/or elbows, jeans too frayed and faded to wear. Put together in the right way, they too can become latter-day heirlooms every bit as valuable as those of the past—not least to your family, who will enjoy pointing out their old school prize day dresses, the birthday frock, or the all-time-favorite shirt or pair of pants. See the projects on the next pages for ideas for making patchwork designs that are simple, modern, and stylish.

Patchwork throw

Patchwork is as complicated as you want to make it. Complex designs using cut out templates and tiny hand-sewn stitches are all very well, but few of us have the time these days. The modern "cheats" approach is to machine-sew together the fragments of fabric, first of all in strips, and then joining the strips of fabric together to form a flat piece of material that can then be cut to create clothing or used to upholster furniture. This eye-catching throw, inspired by a piece by stylist Kristin Perers (see Directory, page 251), uses strips of worn and faded denim, striped ticking, and the edges of vintage linen tea towels. Far easier than re-upholstering a sofa, it's a great way to put to use the parts of pairs of jeans too worn to wear, or the unsullied borders of singed or stained tea towels, which can be picked up cheaply in second-hand stores.

You will need
- Assorted pieces of denim, ticking, and tea towels
- Cotton thread for machine sewing
- Old sheet, blanket, or length of fabric

To make
♥ Choose which pieces of fabric you are going to work with. You want a good distribution of colors, stripes, and textures throughout—it will always show if you run out towards the end and have to start again with new material.

♥ Cut strips and squares of random length but more or less the same width—here they are 6–8 in. On the throw in the photograph, the stripes face the same way on alternating strips, so if you want to do the same thing, divide your fabric into two equal piles and arrange them so that the stripes are vertical for one half and horizontal for the other.

♥ Sew them together in strips in a well-spaced yet random-looking order, with all the stripes facing the appropriate direction. Make enough strips to join together to form the throw.

♥ Pin or tack the strips together, with stripes facing upwards one row, crossways the next. Sew together.

♥ Trim the seams, trimming away large overlaps where necessary, and iron into shape.

♥ Make a backing using an old sheet or blanket or, if you have it, a large length of striped canvas or similar, of contrasting or coordinating colors. Cut this to the same size as the patchwork piece, place right sides together, and sew around the edge, as if making a huge cushion, leaving a little gap along one edge. Turn right sides out through this gap, sew up, and iron into shape. With any leftover fabric, make a couple of cushion covers to match.

This eye-catching throw uses strips of worn and faded denim, striped ticking, and the edges of vintage linen tea towels.

Denim
chair

Old denim jeans are great for patchwork, as the flies, pockets, and worn and faded patches all add interest. Cutting up a pair of jeans and sewing the bits together to make a flat piece of fabric can be the basic starting point for any number of projects, from cushion covers to simple upholstery. This director' s chair was covered in this way, and is incredibly effective, looking much more complicated to make than, in fact, it is.

You will need

◆ A director' s chair that has seen better days
◆ Sandpaper and wood treatment (optional)
◆ Pair of old denim jeans or denim cut-offs
◆ Cotton thread for machine sewing
◆ Hammer and nails or staple gun

To make

♥ Remove the sling seat and back from an old director' s chair and keep as a pattern piece. If the wood is worn or stained, you can sand it down and, if necessary, re-varnish at this stage.

♥ Cut up the denim jeans or cut-offs into pieces that are a similar width but of varying lengths. Stitch together to make two flat pieces of fabric, each roughly the size of the seat and back pieces you have removed. Depending on the size and condition of the jeans, it may be possible to create quite large pieces (as in the photograph) with not too much sewing involved. Allow ¾ in extra at the top and bottom edges to hem and at least 3¼ in at the sides for attaching to the chair frame. The easiest way to stitch together the denim pieces is using a sewing machine to first make strips and then sew them together. Trim the seams to neaten.

♥ When deciding which piece of fabric is going where, keep in mind where interesting features on the jeans will appear on the finished chair—we used the fly detail for the back and a pair of pockets for the seat. Make sure the seat, in particular, is made from strong, unworn pieces, as it will be taking the most weight.

♥ Turn over the top and bottom edges of each patchworked piece and hem by hand or machine, using the original seat covers as a guide.

♥ Wrap the edges around the chair frame so that the raw edges are hidden, and then nail or staple the back and seat securely into place.

Child's
summer dress

We both grew up wearing pretty floral dresses like the one pictured opposite, and Elspeth's mother has continued the tradition by making two summer and two winter dresses from patterns such as this one for every year of her granddaughter Mary's childhood. With simple classic childrenswear coming back into fashion, dresses such as this change hands for large sums of money in stores, but are not difficult for someone with a modicum of dressmaking experience to run up. As the pieces are so small, they can be cut from items of adult clothing—a pretty skirt, for instance—that are damaged in places or no longer worn. Using a contrasting or coordinating fabric for the bodice lining and choosing a colorful button from your button jar for the shoulder strap are unusual touches that make each dress unique. The pattern on pages 238–9 can be made up in two sizes to fit an average one- or three-year-old.

You will need

◆ Pattern from pages 238–9 scaled up on to pattern paper or newspaper
◆ Main fabric:
   Age 1: 43 in x 45 in wide cotton or
   39in x 60in wide cotton
   Age 3: 50 in x 45 in wide cotton or
   39 in x 60 in wide cotton
   Lining:
   Ages 1 and 3: 50 cm (20 in)
   or cut pieces from an old item of clothing
◆ Cotton thread for sewing machine
◆ Button from button tin measuring ¼ in (Age 1) or ½ in (Age 3)

To make

♥ Cut out the dress pieces as directed on the pattern-pieces (these allow to a ½-in seam throughout), placing the front and back skirt pieces and bodice front (optional) against a fold of fabric. For the bodice, cut two pieces each of front and back, one of fabric and one of lining. Cut two straps (optional). With right sides facing, pin the left shoulder seam of the bodice and sew. Repeat with the bodice lining, sewing the left shoulder seam.

♥ With right sides together, pin the main bodice fabric to the lining, matching up the sewn left shoulder seam. Sew around the left armhole. Beginning at the back right armhole, sew around the back armhole across the shoulder seam, around the neck back and front, and around the front armhole.

♥ Trim the seams using sharp scissors and clip around the curved edges to help the bodice lie flat when turned. (You can also machine around the seams using a zigzag stitch to prevent the seams fraying.) Turn to the right side by pulling front through at left shoulder. Iron the seams flat.

💜 For the straps, if using, fold the strap pieces in half lengthwise, right sides together. Sew around the two sides, allowing for a ½-in seam. Trim the corners, then turn to the right side using a knitting needle, if necessary, to push out the corners. Press with a steam iron.

💜 Pin the straps to the front side seam of the bodice, matching the raw edge of the strap to the side of the bodice, approximately ¾-in from the bottom edge.

💜 Place the front and back pieces right sides together and matching the underarm seam, and sew the lining side seam, across the underarm seam, and then the bodice seam, which catches in the side strap. Repeat on the opposite side.

💜 Make a horizontal buttonhole on the back right shoulder, to fit your button (see pages 226-7). Sew either on the sewing machine or by hand with blanket stitch (see page 225). Sew the button on to the back shoulder.

💜 To make up the skirt, stitch the front to the back side seams. Then make two parallel rows of gathering stitches (long running stitches, see page 226) at the top edge on the front and back to within ½ in of the side seams. Pull gently to make the gathers the same width as the bodice.

💜 With right sides together, matching side seams with the side seams from the main fabric only, tack the two pieces of the dress together, then sew on or just below the gathering stitches. Trim and finish the join between bodice and skirt with zigzag stitch and press the seam upwards.

💜 Press under the raw edge of the bodice lining by about ½ in and hand sew with over stitch (see page 226) the folded edge below the stitched line of the gathered skirt to bodice, so hiding the stitch line. Press with a steam iron.

💜 Mark the finished length and trim evenly, allowing about ¾ in to turn up and press all around. Then press under approximately ¼ in along the raw edge and stitch the hem either by hand or by machine.

With simple classic childrenswear coming back into fashion, dresses such as these change hands for considerable sums of money in the stores...

Tea towel
apron

SOME TEA TOWELS seem too good for wiping dishes, so why not make one into an apron? This idea is simplicity itself, as it utilizes the ready-finished edges of the tea towel, meaning that there are only a few raw edges to be hemmed. The apron in the photograph was made using a vintage French linen tea towel; you can buy similar ones on eBay or pick them up from antiques markets or junk shops (see Directory, page 242). Any design with an attractive stripe or pattern could be used, though—even a souvenir cloth from a favorite place.

You will need

- Large tea towel measuring 24½ in x 33 in for an average-sized adult; use a smaller one for a child
- White cotton thread
- 3 yd cotton tape
- Metal D-ring (optional)

To make

♥ Cut off the top corners of your tea towel so that, when sewn together along their diagonal sides, they form a square. Tea towels vary in size, but for this one, the cuts were made 7 in along the top and down each side, leaving 10½ in (unhemmed) for the neckline.

♥ Turn over the raw edges of the main tea towel twice, press with a steam iron, and hem by hand.

♥ To make the pocket, tack together the diagonal sides of the two cut-off triangles, right sides facing, making sure to match any stripes or patterns where you can. Carefully machine stitch together.

♥ Iron out the seam, fold over the raw edges of the pocket square once, and hand hem the one that will form the top of the pocket. Pin or tack the pocket into position on the front of the apron and top stitch by machine, finishing securely at all the corners.

♥ To finish, cut the cotton tape into three: two ties of 42 in each and a neck loop of 24 in. Sew securely into position, using the metal D-ring to make the neck loop adjustable, if required. Press with a steam iron.

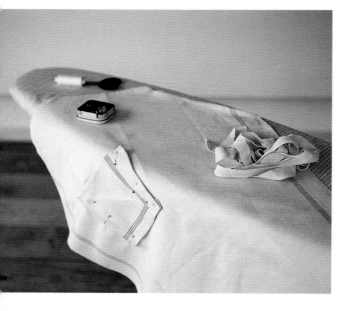

Customizing T-shirts

CUSTOMIZING T-SHIRTS is enormous fun and can make an enjoyable project for children of all ages. With just a little effort and ingenuity a plain T-shirt can be transformed into a unique and covetable item. You can sew, embroider, or appliqué our designs, should you want, but can also be achieved ultra-simply, without sewing—either painting them or using fragments of fabric applied with iron-on webbing. With parental supervision, they would make a great project for a children's birthday party, doing away with the need for a party favor.

You will need

◆ A plain T-shirt
◆ Pieces of scrap fabric
◆ Fusible fabric

To make

Decide what you want to have on your T-shirt—it could be a name, an image, or a slogan; anything is possible. Iron your fabric to the bond paper, then draw your design on to the paper side (remember to reverse the image, if necessary, or the letters if spelling out a name).

♥ Cut out your design, remove the paper backing, and simply iron your fabric on to the T-shirt.

Variations

For a painted T-shirt, either you or a child can paint or draw a design on to the T-shirt using fabric paints or fabric crayons (see page 28 for tips on copying images or lettering).

Restoring
a garden table

THE STYLE QUEEN Nancy Lancaster once likened white plastic garden furniture to "pill packets on a lawn"—and much of the wooden furniture currently available is just as unsightly, not to mention un-ecological. Why buy expensive new items anyway when you can restore old pieces easily enough yourself? You can pick up old metal café tables pretty cheaply from junk shops and antiques fairs—this one was found in a dumpster, covered in rust.

You will need

◆ Metal café table in need of restoration
◆ Stiff wire brush
◆ Sandpaper or electric hand sander
◆ Rust-resistant primer
◆ Paintbrush
◆ Outdoor eggshell paint (see Directory, page 242)

To make

♥ With the stiff wire brush, remove any loose paint and rusty fragments from the table. Smooth over with sandpaper or, if the top is particularly rusty, use an electric hand sander as the best way to achieve an even surface. Wipe with a damp cloth and leave to dry.

♥ Place the table on old newspapers to catch any drips and treat it with rust-resistant primer—the stuff used for car bodies is fine if you have some spare. Take care to brush into joints, hidden nooks and crannies, or decorative features. Leave the primer to dry.

♥ Give the table a lick of paint. Two coats of outdoor eggshell should be enough to give it a good finish. Choose a color that complements the paintwork of your house as well as the plantings in your garden—soft grays, off-whites, and blue-greens all look good outside.

♥ Paint other pieces of old furniture in the same color or use varying shades in the same tonal range.

Renovating a garden chair

OLD FOLDING CHAIRS are ideal for garden seating because they are light enough to move about easily and can be folded up and stored away when not needed. They can be picked up cheaply at junk shops and antiques fairs and restored without too much trouble or expense. It is worth building up a collection, keeping a few out year round and stashing the rest in the shed to bring out for an alfresco lunch or party. Don't worry if they're not exactly the same—painting a motley mix of shapes and sizes all the same color will have a unifying effect. Or if you are lucky enough to find a matching set, from an old school or bandstand, perhaps, try painting them in different shades of the same color-group—smoky blue-grays and mauves, for instance, or olive green through gray-greens to brown. Padded cushions tied on to the frame (see overleaf) stylishly complete the effect.

You will need
- Folding chair in need of renovation
- Stiff wire brush
- Fine sandpaper
- Rust-resistant primer
- Paintbrush
- Wood glue
- Outdoor eggshell paint (see Directory, page 242)

To make

♥ With the stiff wire brush, remove any loose paint and rusty fragments from the chair and then smooth down using fine sandpaper. Wipe with a damp cloth and leave to dry.

♥ Place the chair on old newspapers to catch any drips and treat any rusty metal parts with rust-resistant primer. Take care to brush into joints, hidden nooks and crannies, or decorative features. Leave the primer to dry.

♥ Check the wooden parts for hardiness and, where necessary, repair any cracked back slats or other small areas of damage with wood glue.

♥ When dry, give the chair two coats of outdoor eggshell paint, taking care to brush along the undersides of the slats and into any other hidden-away areas. You may have to touch up the chair slightly in places where the folding mechanism gets in the way.

Outdoor tie-on cushion

GIVE OLD FOLDING CHAIRS (see page 80) or other garden seating a lift with smart tie-on fabric cushions. Choose a hardwearing material, such as canvas, striped cloth, or even oilcloth (see Directory, pages 242–4) in a pattern and shade that goes well with the color of your furniture, as well as the flowers in your garden. A mismatch of various vintage fabrics looks lovely, so raid your scrap box for possibilities. For the ties, you can buy cotton tape from men's clothing stores, but the paper carrier bags given away free in many stores often have tape handles in attractive colors that can be removed and saved for such a purpose (see also Wrapping presents on page 206).

You will need

- Cushion pad or thick foam cut to size
- Hardwearing fabric (see above)
- Sewing thread to match fabric
- 32-in tape or ribbon

To make

- This cushion has an envelope-style opening like the one on page 135. Cut three pieces of fabric: one the size of your cushion plus a ¾-in seam allowance (Piece A) and two that each measure two-thirds of the length of the cushion plus seam allowance (Pieces B and C). Pieces B and C will ultimately overlap each other on the back of the cushion to form the opening for inserting the pad. You may want to cut out Piece C with the selvedge forming the open edge.

- Hem the unfinished edge of B that will form part of the opening (and C, too, if you haven' t made use of the selvedge).

- Cut four lengths of tape or ribbon 8-in long each for the ties.

- Lay out your pieces with Piece A on the bottom (right side facing up), followed by Pieces B, and then C on top (right sides facing down) so that they overlap, pinning two ties between the layers of fabric at each of two adjacent corners so that the ends of the ties are trapped between the seams.

- Sew around the four sides. Turn the cushion cover out so the right side is visible, iron the seams flat, insert the cushion pad, and use the ties to attach to the back of the chair.

Recycled
containers

USING RECYCLED CONTAINERS is a great way to bring individual style to your garden, without costing the earth. From large wooden crates to old wicker baskets down to tiny cookie tins, there are containers of every size, type, and material just waiting to be given a new lease of life as planters. It is all a matter of seeing things with new eyes: Could that old metal trash can cast out on the street by a neighbor become home to a small apple tree on an urban terrace or balcony? Could that holey old watering can be planted up with white petunias? Even toy trucks and boats can be planted up with shallow-rooted plants, such as succulents, to bring a quirky touch to a children's play area. Take inspiration from thrifty gardeners in Greece, India, and Cuba and plant olive trees in large empty olive oil cans or use everything from old buckets to chipped china as containers for edible or ornamental plants. (See Directory, page 242 for places to find salvaged containers.)

Late summer fireworks

Old fire buckets (see opposite) are a great choice for the hot fiery colors of late summer flowers, such as dahlias, crocosmias, and heleniums, offset by dark and bronzy ornamental grasses. Some of the buckets are rounded at the bottom, so you can use the handle to turn them into pretty hanging baskets. Unless they are really rusty, the buckets may need to have extra drainage holes made in the base.

Seaside special

Paint old tires and use them as containers—or why not use a container made from recycled rubber, such as this one (see right)? Given good drainage and planted up with sun-loving plants like ornamental grasses, small scabious, and thrift (*Armeria maritima*), a container like this is perfect for a seaside garden or an exposed urban roof terrace, where the grasses can swish about in the wind.

Take inspiration from thrifty gardeners in Greece, India, and Cuba and plant olive trees in large, empty olive oil cans...

A mismatch of found and recycled objects (see right) can look charming in a garden. But if the make-do-and-mend aesthetic isn't what you had in mind, don't worry. Giving a motley collection of objects a coat of paint in a unifying color will instantly make them look much smarter, and it's up to you whether you choose a bright indigo blue, such as that in Yves Saint Laurent's famous Majorelle Gardens in Morocco, or lower-key gray-greens and blues.

The good news is that recycled objects often already have ready-made drainage holes in the form of rust holes, gaps, and cracks. If they don't have sufficient drainage, the plants won't thrive, so carefully knock or drill more holes, using masking tape around the hole to protect more delicate materials. If metal pots, such as buckets, have a lot of rust, treat them with rust-resistant primer first (see page 78 for instructions). If edible plants are to be grown in the pots, it is advisable to line them first (see page 50 for instructions). Then fill base of the containers with at least 1 in of gravel to further improve drainage and provide some weight for anchoring lighter pots in place.

Pineapple lily

An old florist' s bucket (opposite) makes a great vase-like container for the unusual late-summer blooms of the pineapple lily (*Eucomis bicolor*). Drill a few holes for drainage in the base of the bucket and fill the bottom with 6 in of gravel—vital for anchoring tall planters such as this in place. A mulch of grit, gravel, or shells on top of the soil keeps weeds down and water in.

Tomato box

Why grow tomato plants in boring black plastic pots when a recycled wooden tomato box (see left) is just as effective and twice as much fun? This is a vintage box, but attractive new ones can be picked up from street markets. Line the box with black plastic to retain soil and water (see page 50), place in a sunny spot, and keep well fed and watered.

Tea for two

An old enamel teapot and caddy and a chipped china jug have been given new life (see left) as planters for flowering verbenas in crimson and mauve. When using a mixture of containers, it often looks smarter to restrict the planting to one or two types of flowers or colors. Old enamelware makes great planters and can often be picked up cheaply if there are rust patches—just drill or hammer a few extra holes in the base.

Drought-proof trough

An unwanted galvanized water-tank makes a witty container for drought-proof plants (see below), which won' t need much watering in hot spells. Combine yellow red-hot pokers (*Kniphofia citrina*) and electric purple *Verbena bonariensis* with creamy heads of achillea as a contrasting horizontal shape. Silvery leaves of lavender at the base are the perfect complement for the weathered gray metal of the tank. This would probably need more drainage holes drilled in the base before use. A mulch of pebbles retains water well.

Mexican
tin lantern

INSPIRED BY THIS wonderful Mexican tin lantern that was a present from a friend (see below), here is a less elaborate, but nevertheless charming, version to make yourself. A string of such lanterns, either lined up along a wall or hung from the branches of a tree, would look fabulous. The pinpricks of light cast lovely shadows, while the tin provides the candle with protection from the wind. For a special birthday, wedding, or anniversary party you could even punch out names, initials, or a personal message.

You will need

- An empty tin can, washed out, with label and lid removed
- Erasable felt pen
- Bradawl or small screwdriver
- Hammer
- Wire for handle
- Tea candle

To make

- The lantern illustrated uses a standard size can, but smaller and larger sizes work well too. It is possible to make the holes directly with a bradawl and hammer, but the following method makes it easier and safer to work with.

- Fill the can with water and place it in the freezer until the water has frozen. Then draw your design on the can with an erasable felt pen. Abstract designs like crosses and zigzags work well as borders, with stars and hearts or even birds or flowers as features around the central body of the can.

- Lay the can on to a non-slip surface, such as a towel, and wedge it in position by rolling the towel towards the can on either side. Alternatively, place in a vice, but be careful not to squeeze it out of shape. Using a large nail or bradawl, hammer holes into the can following your design. Place the finished frozen can into the sink to thaw.

- To make a hanging lantern, punch an additional hole on either side near the rim and add a wire handle, twisting to secure in place.

- Place a tea candle in the base of the tin. For added safety, particularly if the lantern is going to sit on a wooden or heat-sensitive surface, sit the tea candle on a small tile or flat fragment of slate or ceramic. Keep an eye on your lantern when lit, and never leave it unattended.

Paper-lined tea candle
holders

Why waste money on fancy tea-light holders for the garden when you can make your own stylish versions from recycled jam jars decorated with old wrapping paper torn into strips, or handmade papers from craft shops (see Directory, page 242)? Get into the habit of saving useful jam jars and experiment with textured Japanese papers that tear to leave an irregular edge, as shown here, or ones that incorporate pressed flowers or skeleton leaves. Papers with a see-through texture or cut out motif work best.

You will need
- Clean, empty jam jars of assorted sizes
- Strips of recycled or handmade paper
- Glue or Scotch tape
- Wire or ribbon for handles
- Tea candles

To make

♥ Cut or tear a strip of handmade craft paper to fit the circumference of each jar, wrap it around the outside of the jar and secure in place using strong glue or Scotch tape.

♥ For handles, bend wire around the rim of the jar and over the top, twisting securely in place. Or use colored narrow ribbon, as here, tying it around the rim, extending one end of the ribbon in a loop over the top and securing it in a double knot on the other side.

♥ Pop a tea candle inside and hang the jars from a pergola or the branches of a tree, making sure there is no foliage directly above the lanterns that could get burnt. Never leave lit lanterns unattended.

Variations

For a variation, cut your own designs from tracing paper and stick them around the jar or paint the glass with glass paint. Threading beads on wire and slipping over the neck of the jar makes a pretty collar.

Experiment with textured Japanese papers that tear to leave an irregular edge.

Summer
bunting

STRUNG FROM LEAFY BRANCHES and blowing gently in a warm breeze, fabric bunting brings a festive air to the summer garden. Good times are here, it seems to say—suggesting parties, village fêtes, and wholesome fun and games. Making your own is much easier than you would think—and means you will always have instant decorations at hand. It's yet another great way to use up odd small remnants of fabric and much-loved old clothes. Make it as long as you like, or sew several lengths to be used in different places. Bunting looks beautiful indoors as well as out, looped along verandahs, draped across doorways, or hung in swags around the walls of a child's bedroom year-round. If you are a member of a craft club, why not make lots of bunting as a communal project and lend it out to each other for parties as required? This bunting is machine-washable and is best kept folded flat in a box between uses to prevent it getting tangled.

You will need

- A mixture of plain, striped, and floral cotton fabrics
- 17 ½ yds colored tape or binding a minimum of ¾-in wide

To make

- Using pinking shears (so that you don't have to hem each piece), cut out 50 triangles, each measuring 8 ½-in wide and deep. Decide on the order of your colored triangles, aiming to get a good mix of patterns and colors.

- Fold the tape in half lengthwise and iron to make a long channel for inserting the triangles.

- Starting about 8 in in from the end of the tape (to leave some free for tying), pin the triangles in position, 4 in apart, opening up the tape and slipping the top of each triangle inside so the raw edge is hidden. Stop 8 in short of the other end of the tape.

- Sew carefully into place all along the length of the tape to secure the triangles in place.

- Making a loop at either end can make hanging easier—and extra tape can be added to extend the bunting or to make it easier to tie on to trees and so on.

Bag-in-a-bag

PLASTIC SHOPPING BAGS are a definite no-no in both the eco-conscious and the style stakes. But finding the right shopping bag—one that's big and strong enough to carry heavy groceries, light enough to fold up small and fit in your handbag, and stylish to boot—is like searching for the Holy Grail. The one featured here checks all the right boxes, incorporating a gusset for extra capacity and a pretty ribbon and button tie for rolling it up small. It's also surprisingly simple to make—choose from striped cotton canvas or pink metallic nylon for a touch of glamour.

You will need

◆ 39 in in any standard width of strong fabric that isn' t too thick or heavy; or use an off-cut measuring 25 x 32 in
◆ Cotton thread for sewing machine
◆ 8- to 12-in ribbon
◆ A pretty button

To make

♥ For the bag, cut out a piece of fabric measuring 32 x 18 in—including a ½-in seam allowance.

♥ To make the straps, cut two strips of fabric, each measuring 21 x 3 ½ in. Fold in ¼ in on each side to the wrong side and iron flat. Then fold each strap in half lengthwise (so that the pattern is on the outside and the folded edges are facing inwards), and machine topstitch all the way along.

♥ For the top edge of the bag, fold in one of the longer sides by ⅛ in to the wrong side. Iron in place and then fold down a further 1½ in and iron again.

♥ Pin the two handles in place, beginning with handle one about 4 in in from the right side edge. Pin one end of the handle, then pin the opposite end about 54 in away from the first end. Have the stitches on the inner side of the handles, and the bottom of the strap pieces level with the bottom of the folded-over edge of the bag (see top picture on page 99). Repeat at the opposite end with handle two.

♥ Secure the handles in place and stitch down the top of the bag with two rows of machine stitching, one about ⅛ in from the top edge and the other along the bottom of the folded-over edge (see top right).

♥ Fold the bag in half, right sides together. Sew the side and bottom seams about ½ in in from the edge. Zigzag stitch over the raw edges to prevent fraying.

♥ To make the gusset, open the bag out so the bottom seam runs down the center and sew a diagonal line of about 4 in across each corner (see below right).

♥ To make the ribbon and button tie, loop the length of ribbon around one of the handles, joining and securing with a button (see left).

♥ To roll up the bag, fold it into three or four sections and roll up, leaving the straps end until last. Then simply wrap the ribbon tie around the roll and wind the loose end of the ribbon around the button to secure.

Finding the right shopping bag is like searching for the Holy Grail...

Beach bag

A GOOD-LOOKING yet practical bag makes a trip to the beach all the more enjoyable. Wider than the shopping bag on page 96 and with longer straps, this bag has been designed to take a large towel and bathing suit, plus picnic goodies, sun screen, books, a hat, and other holiday paraphernalia. Lining the inside with toweling makes the bag extra useful for carrying damp swimsuits back from the beach. We used an old towel that still had plenty of wear left in it but was a bit frayed around the edges. With enough left over, you could also line the shoulder straps with toweling to make them more comfortable. The instructions for the beach bag are similar to those for the shopping bag, but the dimensions are different.

You will need

- 1 ¼ yd in any standard width of strong cotton or canvas-type fabric (we used gingham); or use an off-cut measuring 45 x 28 in
- Toweling: same size as the main fabric—an old towel would be perfect
- Cotton thread for sewing machine
- Tapestry wool
- Recycled rope, shells, and anything else you have on hand to decorate

To make

♥ For the bag, cut two pieces measuring 45 x 20 in, one in the main fabric and the other in the toweling. Place wrong sides together and use as a single piece, tacking together if necessary.

♥ For the straps, cut two strips of the main fabric, each measuring 27 ½ x 4 in.

♥ Make up the bag using the instructions for the Bag-in-a-bag on page 96.

♥ To decorate, stitch an anchor (see page 240) or other seaside image on to your bag using chain stitch (see page 225). We used tapestry wool rather than embroidery thread as wool really stands out, and then added a rope-like piece of trimming recycled from a carrier bag. Add shells and other beachcombing finds, strung like fashionable chains or trophies from the straps (see the Beach sculpture or mobile overleaf for further inspiration).

Beach sculpture or mobile

BEACHCOMBING IS A GREAT pastime, especially for those people who find it hard to sit still. Apart from the fact that it is not often hot enough to lie and bake in the sun, many people find it hard to remain still and would far rather be doing something creative with their time. The rhythm of the tides is endlessly fascinating, and a walk along the shoreline at low tide can be both relaxing and inspiring as the sea breezes blow any worries away, while the flotsam and jetsam may well provide ideas for things to make.

Everyone from toddlers upwards seems to collect buckets or pockets full of seaside finds, so why not make something beautiful or useful with them, rather than leaving them lying around the house gathering dust? This beach sculpture or mobile was made from beachcombings from Cornwall and was inspired by something similar made from shells and lengths of fishing wire by Ros's brother, Mike Badger. Follow the instructions given below, or go on your own tack, inspired by whatever you find. The result is now hanging on the sitting room wall as a permanent reminder of a great summer holiday.

You will need

- ◆ Shells and stones with holes through them (limpet shells with the pointy tops knocked off them are often found in rocky coves and bays, or tiny white conches that look lovely grouped on a table at home)
- ◆ A length of fishing line (we found one washed up with the decorative sparkly flies still attached)
- ◆ A piece of driftwood

To make

♥ Tie a knot in one end of the fishing line and thread on the shells in whatever order works best for you.

♥ When the shell chain is long enough, tie a knot in the other end of the line to secure your finds and attach to a length of driftwood.

Variations

This could also be used as a bell or light pull (see instructions for the Button light pull on page 168). To make a beach mobile, tie small groups of shells on to lengths of rope or fishing line (preferably beachcombed) and hang from either end of a piece of driftwood. This would look particularly good in a beach hut.

Other uses for beachcombing finds include the Razor shell candleholders on page 124.

Summer salad
trough

YOU DON'T HAVE to have an allotment to grow your own food—a windowsill or even a sunny spot on an outdoor table will do. This recycled metal pig trough makes a great container, and is filled with plants that taste and smell as good as they look. Growing the strawberries off the ground like this helps protect them from hungry slugs and snails, allowing them to ripen quickly in the sun. The different species of basil, mint, and sage that have been used add color and aroma to the mix—chocolate mint goes well with strawberries, while some people swear by basil to bring out the flavor of the fruit. Threaded throughout, jaunty "Jackanapes" violas not only pick up the burgundy in the leaves of the basil but can also be eaten. For an unusual and attractive pudding, pick your strawberries, choose a herb to chop or tear over the fruit, and sprinkle with sugar and viola leaves.

You will need

- A salvaged pig trough or other small window box
- Black trash bag (optional)
- Gravel
- General-purpose potting soil
- 5 large strawberry plants
- 3 mint or sage plants—here chocolate mint, lime mint, and tangerine sage
- 3 viola "Jackanapes" or similar
- 3 purple-leafed basil plants

To make

Line the planter if necessary (see page 50) and then add a 2-in drainage layer of gravel to the base of the trough. Add potting soil until the soil in the tallest pots is level with the top of the trough.

Knock the plants gently out of their pots, then line the strawberry plants along the front and shorter sides of the trough and fill in with herbs and flowers in a roughly symmetrical arrangement. Add more soil between the plants so that everything is firmly bedded in.

Keep the soil moist for juicy fruit and luscious leaves—this may mean watering every day in hot spells.

Provide extra slug protection by setting the trough on sheets of sandpaper or special slug-proof mats.

Colorful
cupcakes

There is something very cheerful about cupcakes, whether beautifully decorated like those in stylish bakeries, or studded with candy by creative kids. Having the ingredients for a basic recipe up your sleeve can provide you with something instant for when friends or relatives turn up unexpectedly; equally they can be a fun rainy-day project for children, and a great last-minute present idea. Bake in advance for a children's party or picnic and let the children decorate their own; line up on a tray and spell out "HAPPY BIRTHDAY," "ANNIVERSARY" or so on, plus the recipient's name; or pack in a pretty box or tin tied up with ribbon, which can form part of the present. The following recipe, which can be made by hand or using a hand-held electric whisk, makes 12 regular-sized cakes. For a professional finish, try not to overfill the cases; the frosting looks better if contained by the paper cases rather than dripping down the sides. There are endless variations for decorating the cakes—see right and overleaf for some ideas.

You will need

- ½ cup butter, softened
- ½ cup granulated sugar
- 2 large eggs
- 1 tsp vanilla extract
- ½ cup self-rising flour, sifted
- 1 tsp baking powder
- ⅞ cup confectioner's sugar
- Juice of 1 lemon
- Food coloring (optional)
- Assorted sugar balls, flowers, sweets, and so on, to decorate

To make

♥ Preheat the oven to 325°F. Line a 12-hole muffin tin with cupcake cases.

♥ Put the butter and sugar in a bowl and, either whisking by hand or using a hand-held electric whisk, cream together until light and fluffy. Beat the eggs in a separate bowl and add to the mixture gradually, along with the vanilla extract. Fold in the flour and baking powder and mix gently together. Spoon into the cases, leaving room for the cakes to rise.

♥ Bake for 20–25 minutes until the tops are golden and firm to the touch. Remove and allow to cool before decorating.

♥ To make the frosting, sift the confectioner's sugar into a bowl and beat in the lemon juice until smooth. Divide into smaller bowls and add coloring, if using, one drop at a time, until the desired shade is reached. Spoon on to the cakes and decorate as much or as little as you want.

There is something very cheerful about cupcakes, whether beautifully decorated like those in stylish bakeries, or studded with candies by creative kids.

Foolproof strawberry
jam

MAKING JAM CAN be gloriously satisfying. It's a great way to use up piles of perishable soft fruit from the garden, farmers' market, or pick-your-own farm. As you pour the jewel-bright mixture into jars, you can feel as if you are preserving the very essence of summer to enjoy in the winter months ahead—provided you can wait that long! But the process can also be plagued by pitfalls, leaving you hot and bad-tempered with a gloopy mess that refuses to set or a stiff goo that cuts like jelly—never anything in between. The following recipe should ensure success every time, however. Using jam sugar for low-pectin fruits such as strawberries definitely helps, as does heating the sugar in the oven first, which reduces the overall cooking time. Slow cooking before the sugar is added and a very intense and short boil afterwards preserves the color and flavor of the fruit as well as providing the best consistency.

You will need

◆ 7 cups strawberries, wiped clean and with the stalks removed

◆ Juice of 1 large lemon

◆ 10 cups jam sugar, heated for 20 minutes in a low-heat oven

◆ Pad of butter

◆ 5 13-oz sterilized jars

To make

♥ Put a small plate in the fridge to cool. Place the fruit and lemon juice in a stainless steel (aluminum can react with acid fruit) preserving pan and heat until the juices run. Crush with a potato masher and cook for 5 more minutes without boiling.

♥ Add the warmed sugar and stir until completely dissolved, still being careful not to boil. Add the butter. Then, increase the heat to maximum and bring to a full rolling boil that cannot be stirred down. Start timing and boil for 4 minutes.

♥ Remove from the heat and test whether it has set by dropping a teaspoonful of jam on the chilled plate, leaving for a minute and seeing if wrinkles form when the surface is pushed with a spoon. If they do, the jam is ready and can be poured into sterilized jars (fresh from a hot dishwasher will do), labeled, and stored. If not, boil up again and test a few minutes later.

♥ If giving your jam away as presents, make pretty cotton covers and secure them with string or an rubber band. Using a print featuring the fruit you have used is a nice touch—this one (see right) was found on eBay.

As you pour the jewel-bright mixture into jars, you can feel as if you are preserving the very essence of summer to enjoy in the winter months ahead...

Fresh-baked
shortcakes

THE WONDERFUL THING about shortcakes is that the minimal effort involved is far, far outweighed by the pleasure they give. Unlike homemade bread, which can take ages to make and is often not a great deal better than a loaf bought from a good baker's, homemade shortcakes are immeasurably superior to anything that can be found in the stores. This is because, to be enjoyed at their peak, they have to be eaten on the day they are made, ideally still slightly warm. Serve with whipped cream and homemade jam (see page 116). Keep the ingredients permanently in your home and you'll never be at a loss to feed unexpected guests in style!

NB: Many recipes specify all-purposeflour, but using self-rising flour instead ensures lovely deep shortcakes with a light, fluffy texture. This recipe makes about 8 large shortcakes.

You will need

- ◆ 1 cup self-rising flour, plus extra for dusting
- ◆ ¼ cup granulated sugar
- ◆ ⅓ cup butter, cold and diced, plus extra for greasing
- ◆ 1¼ cups milk, plus extra for glazing
- ◆ 1 egg, beaten

To make

♥ Preheat the oven to 425°F. Lightly grease a cookie sheet and dust with flour. Sift the flour into a large bowl, stir in the sugar, and then rub in the butter until the mixture resembles damp sand. Add the milk and egg and mix briefly to bring it together.

♥ Turn the mixture out on to a floured surface and knead lightly to form a dough. Roll out to a thickness of at least 1 in —this is the secret of well-risen shortcakes. Cut out the shortcakes using crinkle-edged cookie cutters (about 2½ in in diameter is a good size) and place on the cooking sheet.

♥ Brush the shortcakes lightly with a little milk and then dust them with flour. Bake in the oven for 10–12 minutes, or until they are well risen and golden brown. Remove them to a wire rack to cool.

Variations

For fruit shortcakes, add ⅓ cup raisins, sultanas, or chopped dried sour cherries and the grated zest of half an orange. For a savory version, replace the sugar with ⅓ cup grated Cheddar cheese and serve sandwiched with unsalted butter and fresh cress.

Razor shell
candleholders

THE IDEA FOR THESE lovely shell candleholders came from a friend, Carolyn Brookes-Davies of the hat shop Fred Bare, who lives near the beach. The natural colors of the shells are beautiful, and turn translucent as the candles burn down inside. For more ideas using natural objects, see the Beach sculpture or mobile on page 102 and the Artichoke candleholders on page 130.

You will need (per candle)
◆ At least 20 razor shells—the more, the better
◆ A tall candle (such as a taper candle)
◆ Twine, string, or raffia

To make
♥ Gather empty razor shells, which can often be found in abundance along beaches at low tide. Wash them well in soapy water to remove any salt, slime, or seaweed.

♥ Take a tall candle, either standard size or wider if you wish—the parchment-colored "church" candles tend to look best and burn well. Holding it upright on a flat surface, gather the shells, curved side outwards, around it until the base of the candle is well covered all the way around.

♥ Tie tightly in place with attractive twine, string, or raffia and stand on an old saucer. Keep a constant eye on your candleholders once lit.

The shells turn translucent as the candles burn down inside...

Empty razor shells can often be found in abundance along beaches at low tide...

Pumpkin
lanterns

PUMPKIN LANTERNS DON'T have to have ghoulish grins and angular eyes. Let your imagination lead you to other attractive designs that are not so associated with Halloween and can be used to bring a warm golden glow to other autumnal festivities. Try piercing swirly patterns with a skewer, in the style of the Mexican tin lantern on page 90, or go for simpler, more geometric patterns such as those shown here. The polka-dot effect was created using an apple corer, which passes easily through the tough skin and flesh of a pumpkin, and the stars in the lid were cut using a sharp kitchen knife.

All a-glow

Creating the lantern itself can be part of the fun, especially if you' ve grown them yourself. A fine crop of pumpkins is a good excuse for an autumn party, and children will enjoy choosing their own pumpkin and carving out a design with an adult' s help. The scooping can be hard work, however, and is best done with a metal spoon with sharp sides; save the pulp to make soup or chutney, and the seeds for toasting in a low-heat oven—as snacks or for sprinkling on salads or pancakes—or for sowing next spring.

Light the finished lanterns and arange in a row along the top of a brick wall or porch steps until it is time for them to be carefully cradled home. Three tea candles to each lantern give a warm flickering glow. A cluster of these lanterns in a variety of different designs adds immeasurably to the atmosphere of any gathering, inside or out. Take care to site holes in the lid directly above the candle flames, or you will get roasted pumpkin—and never leave lit lanterns unattended.

A fine crop of pumpkins is a good excuse for an autumn party.

Artichoke
candleholders

USING NATURAL OBJECTS around the home brings the beauty and energy of the beach, garden, or countryside indoors. These simple yet stylish candleholders are a great way to exhibit beachcombing finds or gone-to-seed artichoke heads from the garden. Inspired by a similar holder made by Francine Raymond of The Kitchen Garden (see Directory, page 250), they take just a moment or two to make, but are so beautiful you'll be sure to get endless comments about them. Cardoons, which are similar to artichokes, also work well. These look great in a line or cluster on a dinner table, where the dried-out heads are illuminated to a lovely old gold by the tea candle inside.

You will need (per candle)

◆ Cardoon or artichoke head
◆ Tea candle
◆ Small tile or fragment of ceramic

To make

♥ Gather some globe artichoke or cardoon heads that have flowered and gone to seed—the larger the better.

♥ Remove each internal "choke" by simply pulling out the fluffy seeds to leave a hollow receptacle surrounded by the dried scaly calyxes.

♥ Pop a small tile or flat fragment of slate or ceramic in the bottom of each artichoke to provide some extra heat resistance, and place a tea candle on top.

♥ Keep an eye on your candleholders once lit and never leave them unattended.

These look great in a line on a dinner table, where the dried-out heads are illuminated to a lovely old gold by the tea candle inside.

Cushion
covers

WHY BUY EXPENSIVE cushion covers when they are dead easy to make and a great way to use up odd pieces of fabric? The ones piled up in the picture use everything from vintage silk scarves to worn linen curtains, an old cable-stitch cotton jersey, and an unwanted woolen blanket. Part of the fun lies in choosing and matching the fabrics. The instructions overleaf are for the blanket cover, where the front and back are in the same material, but using a contrasting color or texture for each side can look very stylish, and allows you to change the look of your room or sofa in an instant by simply turning over the cushions. For instance, the silk scarf cushion at the bottom of the pile has a back made from luxurious soft pink velvet, chosen to pick out one of the colors in the floral pattern. Try mixing knitted cotton or linen (from an old summer jersey) with a woven linen stripe, felted cashmere with slub silk, or even suede (from the back of an old jacket) with sheepskin or sequins.

Be sure to use a machine stitch that suits both fabrics (if using more than one) without pulling, or sew together (right sides facing) by hand. The instructions given in the overleaf show how to make an envelope opening, but if you want a "two-sided" cushion, make the cover in three pieces (see instructions for the Outdoor tie-on cushion on page 82, omitting the ties), sew up by hand at one end, and unpick for washing.

Recycling blankets

The blanket cushion cover is a good way of using an unwanted blanket or one that has been stained or damaged in parts. If it' s been moth-eaten, kill off any remaining moths or eggs by dry cleaning or leaving overnight in the freezer. If there is a stripe or pattern in the blanket, work out where you would like this on the cushion. You can also make use of edges already finished in blanket stitch or ribbon edging.

You will need

- An old blanket or large sweater
- Cushion pad
- Wool for blanket stitch (optional)
- Strong cotton thread for sewing machine
- Buttons or tapes for opening (optional)

To make

♥ Starting from a finished edge, cut a length of fabric two-and-a-half times longer than the cushion pad, plus 1 in all around to allow for seams. Hem any unfinished edges or fold over and edge with blanket stitch (see page 225).

♥ Fold the fabric, right sides together, as if wrapping around a cushion, so that the edge that you want visible for the outer side of the envelope comes two-thirds of the way up the length of the cushion. Make sure, too, that this edge is inside, facing downwards, with the other flap over the top.

♥ Sew or hand stitch securely along the two outside edges of the cover, sewing through two and then three layers of fabric. Turn the cover inside out, iron if required, and insert the cushion pad.

♥ Sew on buttons or tapes to fasten the opening if required.

Try mixing knitted cotton or linen (from an old summer jersey) with a woven linen stripe, felted cashmere with slub silk, or even suede (from the back of an old jacket) with sheepskin or sequins.

iPod
cover

IPOD COVERS are all the rage and are sold for high prices in shops. But it is easy for even novice knitters to make their own and customize to their own designs. These make great presents for both sexes and all ages; simply vary the color and design to suit. The instructions below include an optional crocheted strap, but if you don't know how to crochet, a pretty piece of ribbon would work just as well.

You will need
- 4-ply cotton, approximately ½ oz (we used mercerized cotton, which has a slight sheen and washes well)
- US size 2 knitting needles
- 2.5-mm crochet hook

Tension over stocking stitch
16 sts and 22 rows = 2 in

Abbreviations
See page 229

Measurements
2 ¾ x 3 ½ in

To make an iPod nano cover
♥ With size 2 needles and the 4-ply cotton, cast on 22 sts and work 8 rows in garter st (knit every row) then work in stocking st (knit one row, purl one row) until the cover measures 6 in.
Work 8 rows garter st and cast off.
Fold the bag in half, right sides together, sew the two side seams and then turn through.

To make an iPod classic or other MP3 player cover
♥ Measure your player and, using the tension guide (see left), work out how many sts you need for the width, then add 4 more sts.

♥ With size 2 needles, cast on the required number of sts and work 8 rows garter st, then work in stocking st until the piece measures twice the length of your player.
Work 8 more rows of garter st and cast off.
Fold the bag in half, right sides together, sew the two side seams and then turn through.

To make the strap
♥ With 2.5-mm crochet hook and the 4-ply cotton, make a 12-in long single chain.

♥ Thread this through the knitted bag just below the garter st top. Alternatively, thread through with narrow ribbon. There is no need to make eyelet holes as the chain st/ribbon can easily be threaded through between the knitted sts. Tie together the loose ends to make a loop.

Tea
cosy

As well as keeping your tea hot, a homemade tea cosy brings an air of warmth and originality to the kitchen table. Choose colors that work with your cups and kitchen décor. For added quirkiness, substitute the embroidered teacup for a message such as "DRINK ME," "AAAAH!" or "THE BEST DRINK OF THE DAY."

You will need

- ◆ About 2 ¼-oz yarn (this was knitted using Aran tweed but any Aran yarn would also work), plus scraps in contrasting colors for the embroidery and pompom
- ◆ Size 7 needles (you can change the needle size to make the cosy larger or smaller; the one pictured fits a six-teacup teapot)

Tension

10 sts and 12 rows = 2 in

Abbreviations

See page 229

To make

♥ With size 7 needles and yarn, cast on 84 sts and work 5 rows to form the border.

Row 1: Knit.
Row 2: Purl.
Repeat these 2 rows once more then divide (work for spout and handle).
Row 5: K42 and keep remaining sts on a stitch holder.
Row 6: K2, p38, k2.

Repeat the last 2 rows 10 times more, ending on a purl row.
Keep these sts on a stitch holder and repeat on the opposite side until the work measures the same front and back. End on a purl row.
Next row: Knit across the whole work.
Next row: Purl.

Then start decreasing as follows:
Row 1: K11, k2tog, * k12, k2tog *, repeat from * to * five times, k1. (78 sts)
Row 2: Purl.
Row 3: K10, k2tog, * k11, k2tog *, repeat from * to * five times, k1. (72 sts)
Row 4: Purl.
Row 5: K9, k2tog, * k10, k2tog *, repeat from * to * five times, k1. (66 sts)
Row 6: Purl.
Row 7: K8, k2tog, * k9, k2tog *, repeat from * to * five times, k1. (60 sts)
Row 8: Purl.
Row 9: K7, k2tog, * k8, k2tog *, repeat from * to * five times, k1. (54 sts)
Row 10: Purl.
Row 11: K6, k2tog, * k7, k2tog *, repeat from * to * five times, k1. (48 sts)

Row 12: Purl.
Row 13: K1, k2tog across work to the last st, k1.
27 sts remain.

♥ Cut your thread and then thread it through all the sts, pulling it tightly.

♥ Use this thread to sew the side seam as far as the opening for the spout, where the 2-st garter st edging finishes.

♥ Sew the bottom side seam to where the 2-st garter st edging begins.

♥ Work your motif (here, a tea cup; see pattern on page 240) using chain st (see page 225) and a contrasting color of wool.

♥ Tack the shape first, if you like, working out from the center of the tea cosy to ensure the motif is central. Work a running st (see page 226) box around the image in a contrasting color of wool.

♥ Make a pompom (see page 152) and attach securely to the top.

Bring back the patch!

DESIGNER CLOTHES ARE EXPENSIVE, and cheap-as-chips high-street items often fall apart after a single season. So it pays to make the clothes that we have and love last longer. These days it is also rather smart—it says you're not a shopaholic, that you care for the environment and have more on your mind than being seen with the latest must-have accessory. Posh people, particularly older ones, are famous for wearing their clothes until they literally fall apart. Care for your clothes by washing only when necessary, using gentle detergents, and protecting from house moths with lavender bags (see page 62), pomanders (see page 174), and pheromone traps. And should the worst come to the worst and a hole or worn patch appear, don't toss it, mend it!

Patching clothes doesn't have to make you look like an extra from *The Waltons*—do it in style and you can wear your patches with pride. If you're handy with a needle, your patches can be objects of beauty. Rather than trying to match the main fabric, make a feature of the patch by using a contrasting color, ideally in a luxurious texture, such as silk or velvet. Turn over the edges and iron and tack into position before machine or hand sewing with small neat stitches. If you want, you can even add a decorative top layer of stitching in a contrasting or eye-catching thread, such as black silk blanket stitch or silver or gold chain stitch (see page 225).

If sewing is not your thing, try hiding the offending hole with a pretty brooch or flower corsage (see page 150). Felt flowers, simply cut with scissors, layered in contrasting or coordinating colors, and secured with a sequin or bead in the center (see also page 146) are all the rage and can look as good on a cashmere jersey as they do on a pair of jeans. Think Sarah Jessica Parker and *Sex and the City*.

It's all a matter of attitude.

Button
power!

THE QUICKEST WAY to update a garment is to change the buttons—either with a matched set or, an eclectic mix of old and new which can be more fun. This vintage jacket had three self-covered velvet buttons, but has been given a quirky contemporary makeover simply by substituting three different buttons all of the same size. The same idea, using a row of smaller buttons, also looks great on a cardigan.

Our mothers always had tins full of old and new buttons all awaiting their moment—a good stash of them makes a wonderful resource. (The contents of a button jar, with a cup cake or muffin tin for sorting the different sizes and colors, can also keep young children amused for hours—though do be aware of the potential danger of babies swallowing and choking on buttons.) Get into the habit of collecting attractive buttons, removing them from clothes that have become too worn to recycle, or picking up nice ones from clothing counters, junk shops, and antiques fairs. It is sometimes worth buying the occasional item from a thrift shop or garage sale simply for the buttons.

Try using your button stash in unusual ways—for instance, the backs of shell buttons are often more interesting than the fronts; or try adding extra buttons between the functioning ones, to make them more of a feature. Buttonholes can always be neatly enlarged to fit a slightly bigger button (see page 227 for how to stitch a buttonhole) or sewn a little smaller to ensure a snugger fit.

For other button ideas, see the Button light pull on page 168, Homemade cards on page 178, and Valentine's heart (worn here as a bracelet) on page 16.

Our mothers always had tins full of old and new buttons all awaiting their moment—a good stash of them makes a wonderful resource.

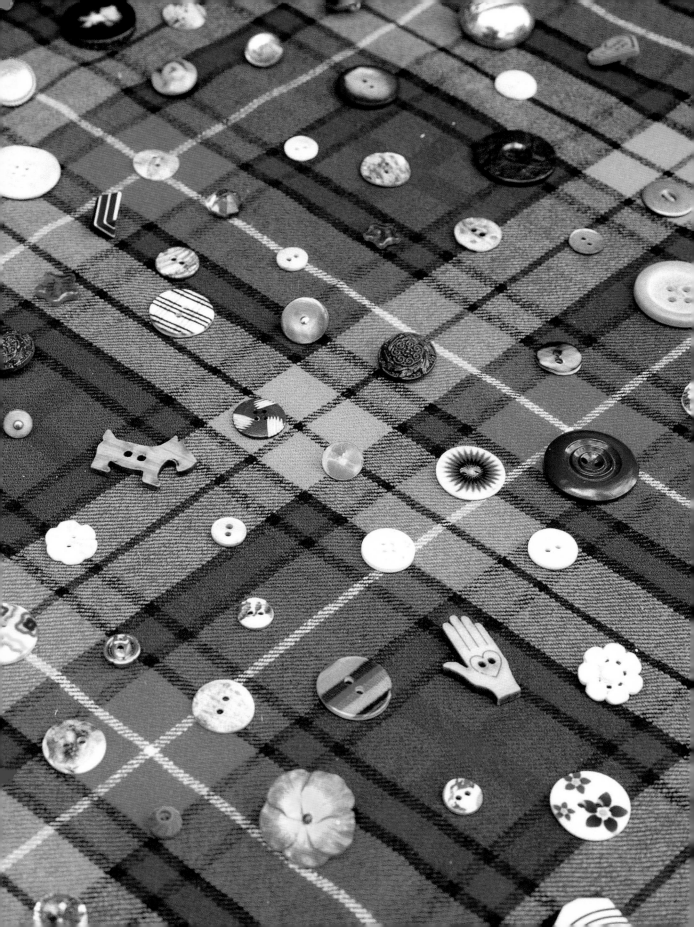

Felt flower hair clips and combs

THESE CHARMING FELT hair accessories are fun and fashionable, and also deceptively simple to make. Children old enough to safely manipulate a pair of sharp scissors should be able to make them with some parental supervision—and they make great presents or items to sell at a school fair.

Flower clip or comb

You will need

◆ Scraps of felt in contrasting colors
◆ Cotton thread in matching colors
◆ Hair clip
◆ Undecorated hair comb

To make

♥ Cut a strip of felt approximately 4 in by between ½ and 1 in, depending on how big you want your flowers. Cut one edge with pinking shears, then with standard scissors cut between each "v" of the pinked edge to approximately ¼ in from the opposite edge (see page 149).

♥ For the flower center, cut a piece of felt in a contrasting color 2 x ¼ in. Roll it up to form the center of your flower and then roll the petal strip around it, sewing the edges and underside securely to hold it all together.

♥ For a simple hair clip, use just one or two flowers (see page 148); if making a comb slide, make five in various colors and sizes (see opposite). Then progress as follows.

♥ For the hair clip, cut a leaf shape in double-thickness felt and sew around the edge with running stitch, with a line down the center to form the leaf vein (see overleaf). Sew the flower to one end of the leaf and then sew the leaf to a hair clip, securing it in three places by sewing over the straight edge of the clip and the underside of the leaf with a small over stitch.

♥ For the comb, cut a piece of felt the width of the comb by ¾ in or double the depth of the top of the comb. Stitch the felt around the top of the comb, sewing between each tooth and also sewing the ends together neatly. Sew the five flowers in a random order on to the felt edge of your comb, stitching from the underneath where it will not show. You can add narrow strips of felt looped over in between the flowers to add more texture or make some small leaves from green felt and sew neatly in place.

Flower corsage

FLORAL FABRIC CORSAGES are back in fashion, adding instant glamour to a party dress or perking up a plain shirt or sweater. This corsage is simple to make, and can be given endless variations by using different colors and textures of old and new fabrics. A group of them would look great on a belt— and they can even be used to hide the odd worn patch or moth hole on a much-loved cashmere sweater (see also Bring back the patch! on page 140). This design was inspired by a corsage seen at a textiles show several years ago and would be a fun project for a crafts club, where an attractive selection could be created in the course of an evening.

You will need

◆ Scraps of fabric in contrasting materials, colors, and patterns
◆ Cotton thread for hand or machine sewing
◆ Brooch pin (optional)

To make

💜 Cut various size circles of fabrics and layer them five or six deep, using a variety of different thicknesses and textures, such as velvet and netting. Use pinking shears for some to give added interest around the edge.

💜 Sew four lines across the diameter of the circles, forming eight segments (see above right), machine or hand sewing as you choose. You can always use silver thread, as shown here, and leave loose strands at the edges by not trimming too close—to add to the overall effect of this piece.

💜 Cut between each line of stitching to just short of the center. Then turn over the corsage and pinch together each segment near the center (below right), sewing each in place to give the flower a three-dimensional shape.

💜 Sew the finished corsage firmly into place; if you want to be able to transfer the corsage from garment to garment, attach a brooch pin to the back.

Pom poms

POMPOMS CAN BE used in all sorts of fun and stylish ways: apart from imparting a jaunty air to hats, they can be added to anything from a tea cosy (see page 138) to a child's toy, or made up in festive colors as Christmas tree or birthday decorations. A cluster of three or five smaller pompoms can transform a child's beanie hat into something rather special, or be attached to cord or lengths of twisted wool to make attractive drawstrings for clothes or children's gloves.

You will need
◆ Cardboard
◆ Darning needle or bobbin
◆ Yarn

To make

♥ Cut two cardboard circles with the diameter of your required size pompom. Cut out a smaller circle in the center (to the proportions shown right).

♥ With the yarn threaded through a large darning needle or bobbin, wind it all around the doughnut shape, tightly and thickly.

♥ When the cardboard is covered and you can hardly get your needle through the central hole, cut the yarn all around the outer edge of the circle and secure by tying another piece of yarn tightly around the center of the pompom.

♥ Remove the cardboard and fluff up the pompom. Trim with a pair of sharp scissors to even it up into a perfect ball. This can also help the edges of the yarn to fluff up nicely.

♥ Attach your pompom securely with matching yarn to whatever you are making.

Autumn chandelier

CREATING SIMPLE AUTUMNAL mobiles using colorful leaves, bright luscious berries, and seedheads suspended from twiggy branches is a great way to make use of the items picked up on a walk in the park or countryside. This elegant autumn chandelier takes the idea one step further, and is only a little more complicated to make. We used scarlet Virginia creeper (*Parthenocissus quinquefolia*) with the fronds of the crimson glory vine (*Vitis coignetiae*) for the base and suspended it from strings of rosehips. Hanging from a tree branch or pergola, it looks especially beautiful when backlit by the low rays of the autumn sun, but could be hung indoors in a hallway for an autumn party. For an evening gathering, you can even wire in tea candles in holders or string candles in glass jars (see also page 92) from the underneath, but take care to leave gaps in the foliage directly above the flames and a good few inches on either side. (In any case, never leave candle flames unattended.) Or just enjoy it on your own, out in the garden on an Indian summer's evening, with a warm throw over your lap and a glass of sloe gin in your hand (see page 162).

You will need
- Ivy or straw
- Plenty of florist's wire
- Brightly colored autumn foliage in reds, oranges, and yellows
- 36 in lengths of string
- Darning needle
- Rosehips, or cranberries for a more Christmassy feel
- Tea candles in glass jars (optional)

To make
♥ Create the base of the chandelier by laying out the ivy leaves (or straw) to make a length of about 1 yd and lashing together by wrapping round and round with the florist's wire. Join the two ends together into a wreath shape and bind together with more florist's wire.

♥ Make a leafy garland by attaching the different foliage and berries using more florist's wire. Work your way around the circular frame, checking for gaps and making sure it is balanced and pleasing to the eye. Individual leaves or small clusters of berries can be added at the end to fill any gaps.

♥ For each berry "chain," thread one end of the string through the eye of the darning needle and thread together the rosehips or cranberries one by one, leaving approximately 4 in of string at either end. When both strings are complete, tie each end to the wreath to form two arcs of berries over the wreath; the point where they cross is where you hang the chandelier from.

♥ To illuminate for evenings, attach tea candles at four points around the chandelier. To do this, remove the wax candles, pierce two holes in the base of each metal case, and attach with florist's wire to the chandelier. Each candle can then be replaced easily whenever the previous one burns out. Just be sure there is no foliage directly above the flame. Alternatively, hang tea candles in glass jars from the bottom of the wreath (see page 92)—these are less likely to blow out in the breeze—but again, make sure the flames are not directly below any foliage.

Spicy pumpkin
soup

SERVED IN A PUMPKIN shell cauldron from which the flesh has been carved, this spicy aromatic soup is ideal festive fare for Halloween and Bonfire Night parties. The cheapest way to acquire a large pumpkin like this is to grow your own—they are spectacularly easy to grow from seed in spring. Just give them a good fertile patch (the top or edge of a compost pile is highly recommended by some people) and plenty of water and watch the fruits swell. For a touch of ghoulish mystery at Halloween, put the lid on the pumpkin as you take it to the table and the steam will creep out through the holes.

You will need

- 5 ½ lb pumpkin (1 lb 6 oz flesh)
- 2 tbsps olive oil
- 1 ¼ cups onions, peeled and sliced
- 1 tsp mustard seeds
- 2 cloves garlic, peeled and crushed
- 1 tsp cinnamon
- 1 tsp cumin
- ½ tsp turmeric
- ½ tsp celery salt (optional)
- 1 ¼ cups carrots, peeled and chopped
- 2 ¼ cups vegetable stock
- Salt and freshly ground black pepper
- ½ cup milk
- Sour cream, to serve

To make

♥ Using a very sharp knife, carefully cut off the lid of the pumpkin about one-third of the way down. Scrape out the seeds and put in the compost or dry them to sow next spring to grow next year' s pumpkins. Scrape out as much of the flesh as you can using a large metal spoon; scraping upwards is most effective. You should end up with about 1 lb 6 oz of flesh, depending on how close you scrape to the skin.

♥ In a large saucepan, heat the olive oil. Add the onions and sauté until clear. Then add the mustard seeds and garlic. Sauté for a further minute and add the remaining spices and celery salt (if using). Mix together and cook for a further minute. Remove from the heat and add the pumpkin, carrots, and stock. Season to taste with salt and pepper.

♥ Return to the heat and bring to a boil. Then reduce the heat and simmer for 20 minutes or until the pumpkin and carrots are soft. Remove from heat and leave to cool slightly.

♥ Purée the soup in a food processor or with a hand-held blender. Add the milk and heat through gently.

♥ When ready to serve, pour the soup carefully into the empty pumpkin shell, add a swirl of sour cream and serve with slices of toast rubbed with olive oil and garlic.

Golden autumn
chutney

IT'S ALWAYS GOOD to have a tasty chutney recipe handy for using up any gluts of fruit or vegetables from the garden—or for cooking up end-of-season bargains from the farmer's market. This all-purpose favorite was passed on from a friend's grandmother who always seemed to be stirring a steaming vat of jam or chutney in early autumn. It has the advantage of being flexible—just vary the main ingredients depending on what you have available. The turmeric gives a lovely golden color, and adding some of the chopped pieces of fruit or vegetable a little later in the cooking makes for a bit of texture—a welcome relief from the dark brown sludge that all too often gives chutney a bad name.

You will need

- 6 cooking or eating apples, peeled, cored, and finely chopped
- 3 lb assorted vegetables including peppers, green beans, and green tomatoes, chopped up small
- 6 onions, peeled and diced
- 1 red chilli pepper, deseeded and finely chopped
- 2 tbsp peeled and finely grated or chopped root ginger
- 1 stick of cinnamon
- 2 tbsp honey or demerara sugar
- 1 tsp allspice
- 1 tsp ground cloves
- 1 tbsp turmeric
- 1 tsp coarse salt
- 4 cups cider vinegar
- 1 lb sterilized jars (see page 233)

To make

- Divide the chopped apples and vegetables into three equal piles. Place two-thirds in a large saucepan or jam-making pot with all of the other ingredients and bring to a boil.

- Simmer for 50 minutes before adding the remaining chopped pieces for a final 10 minutes. Remove the cinnamon stick and pour the chutney, using a funnel, into the sterilized glass jars. Close the lids tightly and label.

Sloe
gin

BLACK WITH A GRAPE-LIKE BLOOM, sloes can be found in abundance in country meadows in autumn. Though bitter to eat, they impart a delicious flavor and jewel-like color to gin when steeped for several months. Treat damsons and blackberries in the same way—and you can always use vodka instead of gin, adding a vanilla pod for extra sweetness. Picking sloes and damsons is more fun if you take an old-fashioned walking stick for gently pulling down the higher branches, where the best fruit is often lurking, just out of reach. The following recipe makes enough for two standard-sized bottles, which can then be divided between several smaller bottles.

You will need

◆ About 1 lb sloes, damsons, or blackberries, well washed
◆ Sugar to taste—most recipes suggest one-third fruit to one-third alcohol to one-third sugar, but this can be too sweet for some
◆ Bottle of cheap gin or vodka
◆ Cinnamon sticks (optional)
◆ Juniper berries (optional)
◆ Almond extract with damsons; vanilla pod with blackberries (optional)
◆ Muslin cloth
◆ Sterilized bottles (see page 233)

To make

♥ Put the washed fruit into plastic bags and place in the freezer for a week, where the cold will break down the skins. This is much easier than the traditional method of pricking the fruit all over.

♥ Fill two bottles or large jars nearly half way (three-eighths) with fruit, add another eighth of sugar to bring it up to half way and then fill to the top with gin. Add a couple of cinnamon sticks or a few juniper berries for extra flavor if you want, and a few drops of almond extract with the damsons or a vanilla pod to the blackberries.

♥ Place the jars where you will remember to shake or swirl the fruit around every other day for a total of two months. When it is ready to bottle, pass the liquid through a doubled piece of muslin several times to clarify.

♥ Discard the sloes—though the soused damsons are good with ice cream—and then, using a funnel, pour into pretty glass bottles you've been saving, and label. The gin is ready to drink after three months, but is best left for a year.

Quince
brandy

IF YOU HAVE a quince tree in your garden, you'll be familiar with that guilty feeling every autumn when, lost in wonder at the sight of their golden beauty, you also don't know *quite* what to do with the piles of fruit gathering on the grass or in bowls and bags around your kitchen. Quince jelly, or *membrillo*, while delicious, is terribly time-consuming to make, involving lots of boiling and straining through muslin. In contrast, this quince brandy is simplicity itself—you don't even have to core and peel the fruit. It can be drunk on its own, added to cocktails, or used to soak dried fruit for fruit cakes or mince pies. In pretty, clear glass jars or bottles, with a ribbon or handwritten label around the neck, it also makes a lovely present. The amount below fills one 5-liter jar or several smaller containers.

You will need
- 4-6 quinces
- 4 bottles cheap brandy
- 3-4 cinnamon sticks
- 6 star anise
- Sterlized bottles or large jar (see page 233)

To make
♥ Wipe the quinces clean and cut them into quarters or large chunks without peeling or coring. Place the fruit in a large clear glass jar and pour the brandy over to cover the fruit and fill to the top.

♥ With a long-handled spoon, carefully push in the cinnamon sticks and star anise so they can be seen from around the edges, and seal with the lid. Leave for at least six weeks before drinking—the longer the better.

Button light
pull

USING AN ATTRACTIVE PEBBLE or favorite button is a great way to add individuality to a boring old light pull. But why stop at just one? Buttons of all shapes, sizes, and colors have been threaded together here to make this stylishly sculptural pull, which feels as good as it looks. You may well already have a button jar packed full of treasures (see page 142). This project is good for using up those buttons that never seem to get chosen over the years, or ones that have been taken off an item of clothing in order to update it with different buttons (see also page 142). For a different look, why not restrict yourself to one or two colors—just white and/or mother-of-pearl would look stunning—to coordinate with the colors you have used to decorate the rest of the room? The same method could also be used for an interior bell pull—inside a porch, for instance.

You will need

◆ Strong string (use string rather than cord, as some of the holes in the button may be small)
◆ Collection of buttons
◆ Scotch tape

To make

♥ Tie a knot at the bottom of the string, winding the thread around two holes in the bottom button for extra security.

♥ Start threading your buttons, varying the mix all the way up, even adding one or two buttons with sideways (shank-back) holes for a quirky touch. Wrapping Scotch tape around the end of the string will prevent it fraying.

♥ Stop where you feel the pull looks good—or when your supply of buttons runs out! You can go right up to the ceiling if you want. Secure the top button with a knot and cut the string, leaving a little spare for tying.

♥ To finish, stand on a chair or stepladder and tie your button pull securely to the cord pull already hanging from the ceiling, trimming the ends neatly.

Victorian
sand pincushion

HERE IS A contemporary spin on a technique that was popular in Victorian times. Pincushions such as this one, decorated with pins pushed in to create elaborate dedications and designs, were made to commemorate births, weddings, and other occasions and were often given as presents. Here, the idea has been revived, but brought up to date by simplifying the design and using a fashionable dark purple velvet for the background. Using sand from a garden center or hardware store to stuff the cushion makes it heavy enough to be used as a bookend or paperweight. And pushing pins through the fabric into the sand is strangely satisfying and absorbing. Using diamante-style pins is a nice touch.

You will need
- Scraps of plain velvet or similar fabric
- Cotton thread for sewing machine
- 2 ½ lb sand for a cushion measuring 7 x 6 ¼ in
- Tissue paper (optional)
- 1 pack of dressmaker' s or diamante-style pins

To make
♥ Cut out two pieces of fabric each measuring approximately 7 x 6¼ in. Place together, right sides together, and sew around the edges with very small stitches so the sand cannot find a way out, leaving a small gap on one edge. To be sure that you avoid sand leaking out, you could always make an inner bag in calico or fine cotton. Trim the corner seams, turn right sides out, iron into shape, and fill tightly with sand. Sew up the opening neatly.

♥ Decide on your design. Work freehand from a drawing or sketch it out on tissue paper, pinning the paper in place and working your design through it on to the cushion and then tearing the paper away afterwards.

♥ Begin sticking in your pins to create the design, working methodically from the middle out, to ensure symmetry.

♥ Be sure to keep the pincushion well away from small children, to whom the pins could be harmful.

Hot-water bottle
cover

THIS COZY HOT-WATER bottle cover is not only a clever way to make use of an old or felted shirt; it's also an improvement on many similar covers that are sold in the stores. By making the opening at the bottom, rather than at the top end of the cover, the danger of damage when stretching it over the stopper end of the bottle is reduced. You can make it from an old blanket or similar thick fabric, but the stretch in the knitting makes an old sweater ideal—it's a great use for one that has holes in elsewhere, or has been felted by washing at too hot a temperature. Felted wool or even cashmere has a lovely texture and is great for this purpose as it won't unravel. Choose one with an attractive edging if possible, taking care when you lay it out to make the natural edge of the sweater the edge of the "flap" in the cover.

You will need
◆ Large piece of paper
◆ Old sweater
◆ Cotton thread to match

To make
♥ Draw around your hot-water bottle, adding ½ in all around for a seam allowance. Then make two paper pattern pieces as follows:

PIECE A must be at least 2 in longer than Piece B and incorporate the natural edge of the jersey at the bottom. PIECE B needs to be approximately ½ in shorter than the hot-water bottle.

Cutting the pattern pieces to these dimensions allows for the longer piece (A) to overlap the base of the bottle and also the shorter piece, thus creating the envelope opening.

♥ Cut out the two pattern pieces from your fabric, being sure to place the bottom edge of each pattern piece along the natural edge of the knitting.

♥ Fold up the bottom 2 in of Piece A, right side to right side, and pin or tack in place at the edges. Then, with right sides facing, place together the two pieces, matching up the tops. Piece B should be about ½ in shorter than Piece A.

♥ Sew around the cover using a small zigzag stitch on a sewing machine or use back stitch (see page 225) if sewing by hand. Do not sew along the folded edge.

♥ Turn right sides out and bring the 5-cm (2-in) fold to the front to create the envelope edge that secures your hot-water bottle in place.

Citrus
pomander

MADE AND USED since Elizabethan times, a pomander is a natural air-freshener and moth repellant that is just as effective today. Tuck some in your clothes drawers and laundry cupboards, hang from closet rails, or stack several in a bowl instead of potpourri. Oranges are most commonly used, but lemons or limes work just as well, their strong aroma mingling with that of the spices. Pomanders take patience to make, but can be an enjoyable project for children—and make lovely Mother's Day presents. They last for many years; if the scent is fading, add a few drops of clove oil to the spice mix and roll the pomanders in it again.

You will need (per pomander)

- Small or medium-sized unblemished citrus fruit
- Masking tape or 2 rubber bands
- 1 oz large-headed cloves
- Fine knitting needle, skewer, or cocktail stick
- Paper bag to fit fruit
- 1 tsp each of cinnamon, nutmeg, and ground cloves or a tablespoon of ready-made mixed spice
- 1 tsp ground orris root (available from healthfood stores—can be omitted, but helps preserve the pomander)
- Ribbon for hanging
- Dressmaker' s pin or PVA glue

To make

♥ Take your fruit and, using masking tape or rubber bands, mark out the space on the fruit where the ribbon will lie. This makes it easier to wrap the ribbon around the pomander once it has dried.

♥ Stick the whole cloves into the fruit, beginning at the navel and working a line all around the fruit, then a parallel line around your ribbon space, keeping to a symmetrical pattern where possible. If the skin seems tough, make holes first using a knitting needle, skewer, or cocktail stick. The cloves need to be fairly close together but not quite touching.

♥ Mix together the ground spices and orris root, if using, on a plate and when the fruit is covered with cloves, roll it in the powder. Place in a paper bag and leave in a dry, dark place for 6–8 weeks. (Do not use a plastic bag as it will prevent the pomander from drying.)

♥ During the drying process, the clove oil should preserve the orange skin, but if you notice any mold or decomposition, throw it out and start again. The pomander is fully dry when it has shrunk and sounds light and hollow when tapped. Shake off any excess spices.

♥ Wrap the ribbon around the fruit, securing with a dressmaker' s pin or PVA glue at the base, and make a loop or bow at the top for hanging.

Homemade cards

MAKING YOUR OWN greetings cards is satisfying on many different levels. It saves money and provides a useful and enjoyable wet-weather activity. It also means that you always have a stash of gorgeous cards to send to friends or relations, whatever the occasion—handmade cards are always appreciated and are usually kept for far longer than store-bought ones.

When it comes to designs, they can be as simple or complex as your time and abilities allow. The very simplest ideas can be wonderfully effective: for instance, the card shown here was created by sticking just one heart-shaped pressed leaf on to a card and writing a short message by hand. This was a morning glory leaf that had just started to turn a deep shade of autumnal copper, picked and pressed between sheets of paper in a large heavy book, with other books left on top to weight it down for a couple of weeks. (If you have an Aga or Rayburn, a good way of pressing leaves is to sandwich them between the sheets of an entire newspaper section and place them beneath rugs in front of the Aga where passing feet will walk over them.)

The other ideas illustrated involve a little sewing—collages of buttons and simple running stitches worked on to colored felt. Cutting out the shapes with pinking shears adds to the decorative effect, and a similar-sized piece can be glued on to the inside front of the card to hide knots and so on. Sewn cards take a little longer, but can be done quite easily while watching television or listening to the radio. Other ideas include recycling old unused photographs of flowers, children, and so on, or snipping around and mounting children's drawings.

Handmade cards are always appreciated and are usually kept for far longer than store-bought ones.

Crochet squares

LIKE KNITTING, crochet has lost its former fuddy-duddy image to become highly fashionable, with designers such as Dolce & Gabbana and Vivienne Westwood sending crocheted dresses and accessories down the catwalks in recent years. Luckily, it is even easier than knitting to learn, and can become quite addictive! Crochet squares, joined together in a funky-colored patchwork, are a perennial favorite—and are also the simplest and easiest way to start. Once you have mastered the basic square, several can be joined together to make anything from a simple scarf or cushion cover to a large double blanket like this one.

Traditionally a way of using up scraps of leftover yarn, patchwork crochet has to be carefully planned if it is not to end up looking a disordered mess. This blanket, bought in a thrift shop, was made in the 1940s by someone who clearly had a sharp sense of color and design. Though each square is random in color and order for the first three rounds (rings of crocheting, starting in the middle of the square, see page 183), it is coordinated with the surrounding squares for the final, outer round—a brown marl for the squares that make up the central panel, then apple green, and finishing with blue for the wide surround that hangs down the bed. This simple discipline really draws the design together—if you look carefully you can see squares using the same or similar colors distributed irregularly but reasonably evenly throughout the blanket. A similar effect could be achieved by working out which yarn you have most of and using it to work the outer round of each of your squares. Turn the page for instructions to start making your very own family heirloom.

You will need

◆ Yarns in assorted colors, but always the same weight (we have used doubleknitting (DK) yarn)

◆ 3.25-mm crochet hook if using DK yarn

Abbreviations

See page 231

To make a single square

This is an easy, basic square for anyone who can crochet. For a good introduction to basic crochet skills, see the books and courses listed in the Directory on pages 245-6. The following makes a square measuring approximately 3 in. Work each round in a different-color yarn.

♥ With 3.25-mm crochet hook and yarn, make 6ch. Join in a circle with a sl st.

ROUND 1: 5ch (count as 1tr and 2ch), 11tr into center, sl st to 3rd of 5ch.

ROUND 2: Sl st into next ch, 5ch (count as 1tr and 3ch), 3tr into same space, * 1ch, miss 3tr (3tr, 2ch, 3tr) into next sp, repeat from * twice, 1ch, miss 3sts, 2tr into same sp as 5ch at beginning of round, sl st to 3rd of 5ch.

ROUND 3: Sl st into next ch, 5ch (count as 1tr and 2ch), 3tr into same sp, * 1ch, miss 3tr, 3tr into next sp, 1ch, miss 3tr **, (3tr, 2ch, 3tr) into next sp, rep from * twice, and from * to ** again, 2tr into same sp as 5ch, sl st to 3rd of 5ch.

ROUND 4: Sl st into next ch, 5ch (count as 1tr and 2ch), 3tr into same space, * (1ch, miss 3tr, 3tr into next sp) twice, 1ch, miss 3tr **, (3tr, 2ch, 3tr) into next sp, rep from * twice, and from * to ** again, 2tr into same sp as 5ch, sl st to 3rd of 5ch. Fasten off.

To sew together squares to make up a blanket

♥ Work as many squares as possible, thinking about your palette as discussed above. Join your squares together with dc by placing squares wrong sides together. Join all squares with the same color throughout the blanket, keeping some aside for repairs.

♥ When the all the squares are joined together, work a border around the edge in the following way:

ROUND 1: Work 3tr 1ch into each space between 3trs of each square edge.

ROUNDS 2 TO 4: Work 1dc into each tr all around blanket. Fasten off.

The border can be worked in a plain color or in different colors for each round, depending on the effect you want and how much yarn you have left.

Cross-stitch
no entry sign

CROSS STITCHING IS PERFECT for long winter evenings, when you want a restful yet creative task. Once you have mastered the basic technique, it can be done while watching an old film on television or talking to a friend. Many habitual cross-stitchers swear by its relaxing, almost meditative qualities: the mind is freed from outside worries but needs to stay present to the task to follow the pattern. Cross stitch is often associated with old-fashioned samplers, and you can easily make your own versions to dedicate a birth or marriage with a design incorporating names and dates and so on.

But why not give cross stitch a contemporary twist? Hand stitching is very much in fashion these days, with designers from Paul Smith to Marni and Dolce & Gabbana incorporating embroidery in their clothes. Instead of traditional designs using flowers, cats, and animals, find inspiration in the artist Tracey Emin's take on needlework (you can see her travel bag on display in the fashion galleries at the V&A Museum in London) and think subversive. There can be charm and humor in the juxtaposition of the painstaking, timeworn techniques and an offbeat, unexpected message: "GO AWAY" on a teenager's door, for instance, or "LEAVE ME ALONE." Here, a simple "no entry" road sign has been fashioned in red thread on a white background: you could add the words, too.

The internet is full of cross-stitch designs that can easily be copied and transfered to fabric (see page 225 for more information on cross stitch and the Directory, pages 243–4, for specialist suppliers).

Striped woolly
scarf

A LONG STRIPY SCARF makes a great addition to any outfit once the weather gets colder. This is just about the most simple scarf ever—perfect for novice knitters and suitable to be worn by men as well as women, of any age. The design uses basic garter stitch throughout and incorporates lots of changes of color, which, if done neatly, can look good on the reverse side, too. This is a great way to use up scraps of wool—just check that they are all of the same weight. Even very short lengths in contrasting colors can be used for the cast-on and cast-off edge, adding an attractive finish. Improvise and make up your own pattern, or stick to the simple instructions below.

You will need
- 200 g (7 oz) chunky yarn in main color (duck egg) (MC)
- Approximately 30 g (1 ¼ oz) chunky yarn in color B (orange) (col B)
- Approximately 30 g (1 ¼ oz) chunky yarn in color C (green) (col C)
- 6.5-mm (US size 10 ½) knitting needles

Abbreviations
See page 229

Tension over garter stitch
The yarn we used worked out at the following tension, but note the needle size and tension on your ball of wool (usually written on the ball band) in case it is different, and change accordingly.
14 sts and 26 rows = 10 cm (4 in)

Measurements
22 x 115 cm (8 ½ x 45 in)

To make
♥ With 6.5-mm needles (US size 10½) and col B, cast on 30 sts.
Rows 1–4: Change to col C, knit.
Rows 5 & 6: Col B, knit.
Rows 7 & 8: MC, knit.
Rows 9 & 10: Col C, knit.
Rows 11 & 12: MC, knit.
Rows 13–16: Col B, knit.
Rows 17 & 18: Col C, knit.
Rows 19–22: MC, knit.
Rows 23 & 24: Col B, knit.
Rows 25 & 26: Col C, knit.
Rows 27–44: MC, knit.
Rows 45 & 46: Col B, knit.
Rows 47–52: MC, knit.
Rows 53 & 54: Col C, knit.
Rows 55–206: MC, knit.
Rows 207 & 208: Col C, knit.
Rows 209–214: MC, knit.
Rows 215 & 216: Col B, knit.
Rows 217–234: MC, knit.
Rows 235 & 236: Col C, knit.
Row 237–238: Col B, knit.
Rows 239–242: MC, knit.
Rows 243 & 244: Col C, knit.
Rows 245–248: Col B, knit.
Rows 249 & 250: MC, knit.
Rows 251 & 252: Col C, knit.
Rows 253 & 254: MC, knit.
Rows 255 & 256: Col B, knit.
Rows 257–260: Col C, knit.
Change to col B and cast off.
Weave in any loose ends.

♥ For a longer or shorter scarf, add or reduce rows between rows 55 and 206.

Fingerless gloves

THESE STRIPY GLOVES are warm and stylish while still leaving your fingers free. The pattern is ideal for using up ends of 4-ply wool—the pair of finished gloves weigh approximately 2 oz. It would be very easy to knit rainbow stripes from this pattern if you have a range of colors to hand. The gloves could also be knitted shorter by reducing the number of rows between rows 33 and 47, or made longer by knitting extra rows before the decreasing starts.

You will need

- ◆ 2 oz of 4-ply wool in mixed colors (here we have used brown, aubergine, and moss)
- ◆ size 3 knitting needles

Key

Color A: brown (col A)
Color B: aubergine (col B)
Color C: moss (col C)

Abbreviations

See page 229

Tension

14 sts and 18 rows = 2 in

Measurements

Finished length is approximately 10¼ in

These stripy gloves are warm and stylish while still leaving your fingers free...

To make the right glove

♥ With US size 3 needles and col B, cast on 59 sts.

Change to col A and work 6 rows in k1, p1 rib.

Dec first at end of row 6. (58 sts) (NB: For decreasing, knit together the third and fourth sts from the edge. This produces a fashioning mark on the gloves, which gives them a more stylish finish.)

Cont with col A.

Row 1 (RS): Knit.

Row 2: Purl.

Row 3: Using col B, knit.

Row 4: Purl.

Row 5: Using col C, knit.

Row 6: Purl.

These 6 rows form the pattern.

Cont in pattern for stripes, dec first at each end of the following row and then on rows 15, 21, 27 and 33, until 48 sts remain.

Cont until the beginning of row 47, then work thumb gusset as follows, keeping stripes correct.

Row 1 (RS): K24, inc in next st, k2, inc in next st, k20. (50 sts)

Work 3 rows.

Row 5: K24, inc in next st, k4, inc in next st, k20. (52 sts)

Work 3 rows.

Row 9: K24, inc in next st, k6, inc in next st, k20. (54 sts)

Work 3 rows.

Row 13: K24, inc in next st, k8, inc in next st, k20. (56 sts)

Work 3 rows.

Row 17: K24, inc in next st, k10, inc in next st, k20. (58 sts)

Work 1 row.

Row 19: K38, turn and cast on first.

Row 20*: p14, turn and cast on first. (15 sts)

Work 6 rows on these 15 sts, keeping stripes correct.

Change to col A and work 2 rows in k1, p1 rib.

Cast off with col B.

Join the thumb seam.

With right sides facing, rejoin yarn, pick up 4 sts from the thumb base (2 either side of seam) and cont to end of row.

Work 16 rows more.

Change to col A and work 4 rows in k1, p1 rib.

Change to col B and cast off.

To make the left glove

♥ Work as right to the beginning of thumb gusset shaping. Then work as follows:

Row 1 (RS): K19, inc in next st, k2, inc in next st, k25. (50 sts)

Work 3 rows.

Row 5: K19, inc in next st, k4, inc in next st, k25. (52 sts)

Work 3 rows.

Row 9: K19, inc in next st, k6, inc in next st, k25. (54 sts)

Work 3 rows.

Row 13: K19, inc in next st, k8, inc in next st, k25. (56 sts)

Work 3 rows.

Row 17: K19, inc in next st, k10, inc in next st, k25. (58 sts)

Work 1 row.

Row 19: K33, turn and cast on first, cont as for right glove from *.

Making up

♥ Sew the side seam with mattress stitch (see Web site recommended on page 228), catching in ends where you can. Then sew in any remaining ends and press lightly with your iron on the wool setting.

Paperwhites on pebbles

FORGET EXPENSIVE IMPORTED cut flowers in winter and fill your house with the fragrance of "Paperwhite" narcissi from November until February. They look especially lovely at Christmas, when the pure-white star-like flowers provide a soothing contrast to the visual cacophony all around—and also make a wonderful present. The bulbs contain all they need to grow, so don't require soil. The flowers take five or six weeks to appear, so to ensure a good a Christmas show, plant them in late October. Each group of flowers will last for a few weeks, so for a continuous supply, prepare successive batches.

You will need

- Glass bowl or dish
- Pebbles, stone chippings, or similar
- "Paperwhite" narcissi bulbs (see Directory, page 247)
- Stick of artist' s charcoal
- Water
- Ribbon or sticks, for support

To make

♥ Fill half the container with pebbles and arrange the bulbs carefully on top—you can cram 20 or more into a large dish for a stunning centerpiece, but just three or four in a smaller bowl will look great as well.

♥ Fill with water just to the base of the bulbs (they rot if fully immersed) and add a stick of artist' s charcoal to the water to stop it stagnating and therefore smelling.

♥ Keep the container in a warm room and sit back and watch as snaky white roots anchor themselves around the stones, and green shoots sprout with buds concealed within.

♥ Flowering should start in five or six weeks—for a continuous supply have several containers on the go, starting a new one every two weeks.

♥ If the stems shoot up too high and become unruly, as often happens, bind the stems with pretty recycled ribbon, or add twiggy sticks or branches of catkins as supports.

♥ Presented in this way, with lots of buds yet to open, "Paperwhites" make lovely Christmas presents—or give them in "kit form" with all the components packed in a box with handwritten planting instructions.

Indoor
hyacinths

As FRAGRANT AS they are beautiful, hyacinths are the perfect indoor bulb for winter. Grown in containers or special "forcing" jars, they also make lovely presents. Unlike most other plants, hyacinths can be grown successfully in pots without drainage holes, enabling you to press anything into use, from old painted mugs to small enamel buckets or vintage soup tureens. Or for presents, pot them up into pretty mugs or salad bowls that can later be washed out and used for their original purpose. Clear glass forcing jars are available from garden mail-order supplies (see Directory, page 248), but the most desirable ones, often in jewel-bright colors, date back to the 1950s and can sometimes be found in antique or junk shops.

To raise your own plants from bulbs, order or buy "prepared" bulbs—which have been bred for early flowering—in late summer. Hyacinths need to be kept for 10–14 weeks in darkness to develop a strong root system and for the buds to appear, so for blooms at Christmas, start by mid-September. White is always a safe and stylish choice, but there are some good dark blues and purples around, such as the amethyst-colored "Woodstock" pictured here.

You will need
◆ "Prepared" hyacinth bulbs (see above)
◆ Multi-purpose compost and florist' s moss and container, or forcing jar
◆ Stick of artist' s charcoal

To make
♥ If planting in soil, place the bulbs on a bed of damp compost and cover with more compost. Then cover with a layer of florist' s moss, leaving only the very tops of the bulbs exposed.

♥ If using a forcing jar, fill the jar with water until the base of the bulb is no closer than ¼ in away from the surface. The mere presence of water is enough to get the roots growing; bulbs rot if left to sit in water.

♥ Add a stick of artist' s charcoal to the soil or water to prevent it stagnating and therefore smelling.

♥ Leave in the dark until the bud is clearly visible between the emerging leaves, checking to ensure the compost never dries out. Flowers should follow in a few weeks.

♥ Alternatively, buy cheap pots or trays of hyacinths in full bud and pot up as above, rinsing the roots carefully if you are using forcing jars.

Christmas wreath

THIS NATURALLY BEAUTIFUL festive wreath is a far cry from the tinselly, gaudy versions available in stores and markets, which are often heavy on dark, gloomy greenery. It is also surprisingly fun and easy to make and will be much admired on your front door for a good two to three weeks. For the cheapest, greenest, and most natural effect, you would ideally forage your own foliage from garden or hedgerow—ivy in particular needs a good annual prune, so you'd be doing it a favor. Or you can buy it all—it's worth making an early-morning trip to a flower market and buying enough to supply a few like-minded friends, too. Why not get a few wreath-makers together for an informal workshop in your house? Fueled by a simple yet delicious supper and a glass or two of wine, much fun will be had and the wreaths will grow, like patchwork quilts, while you chat and work.

You will need

- Whippy willow branches
- Trailing ivy
- Roll of florist's wire
- Holly leaves
- Holly or other red berries
- Pine cones
- Mossy twigs
- Hydrangea head—the redder the better
- Strong ribbon or string for hanging

To make

♥ Lay out the whippy willow branches to the desired circumference for your wreath. Lay long strands of ivy on top of it and lash all layers tightly together with the florist' s wire to make a long sausage of foliage. This gives your wreath a good solid base and will help keep a strong round shape. (It' s possible just to use holly and ivy as a base, but you may find that the weight of larger wreaths will cause them to stretch into an oval when hanging.)

♥ Form the sausage into a wreath shape and secure the ends together with wire. This makes the base of the wreath.

♥ Then, working around the wreath, attach holly leaves, berries, cones, twigs, and sections from the hydrangea head, and any other Christmassy foliage, evenly around the circumference, securing each with the florist' s wire.

♥ When you have gone round once, hang the wreath to view from a distance, and continue to add more leaves and berries if any part looks sparse.

♥ Attach a length of strong ribbon or string at the top back of the wreath where it will not show, for tying around a nail or hook on your door.

♥ The wreath should last a good three weeks if hanging outside and may even dry out sufficiently to carry on as an indoor decoration, to be supplemented with seasonal flowers and foliage, throughout the rest of the year.

Advent
calendar

MADE FROM AN old linen sheet with 24 hand-painted pockets, this beautiful advent calendar is a cut above the disposable commercial ones available in the shops. Reusable year after year, it has the scope to become a family heirloom handed down through the generations. This is a project a whole family or school class could work on together—each person choosing a number of pockets to decorate. Or, if you want a more uniform look, you could do as we did and ask a talented friend (in our case the artist Mary Mathieson) to paint the entire design. The joy of it is that you can put whatever you like in the pockets: chocolates are by no means out of bounds (we used them here), or you could use small toys, pieces of a nativity scene that then get built up elsewhere, or other treasures. The pattern below uses a sewing machine but the project could be done by hand.

You will need

◆ An old sheet, or plain linen or cotton, at least 32 x 50 in or 50 in of 36 in wide fabric if buying specially
◆ Fabric paints and fabric crayons
◆ Assorted cotton threads for machine sewing
◆ Piece of dowelling approximately 30 in
◆ Ribbon for hanging

To make

♥ From the fabric, cut a piece measuring 29 x 32 in. Then cut out 23 smaller pieces of various sizes for the pockets.

Six pieces each of the following sizes:

4½ x 4½ in
4½ x 5 in
4¾ x 4¾ in

Five pieces measuring:

5 x 6 in

Then, finally, one piece measuring:

6 x 6 in for the central Christmas Eve pocket.

♥ Using the fabric paints and fabric crayons, decorate each piece with a number from 1 to 23 and other Christmas images, if you like, perhaps using favorite cards or images from the internet for inspiration. Decorate the 6 x 6 in piece with a special image for Christmas Eve—we painted an angel.

♥ Make sure to leave at least ½ in around the image on all sides for hemming and attaching to the background.

♥ When all the small pieces are decorated, fold over ½ in along the top of each one, press, and then hem with a contrasting-colored thread. We chose a stitch on the sewing machine from the embroidery settings (nothing complicated as the sewing machine is 40 years old), but it looks very effective (see above). You might find other possibilities.

♥ Carefully fold in the three other sides on each piece by ½ in and iron to hold (see opposite). They are then all ready to attach to the background piece.

♥ Pin each pocket randomly on to the large piece, mixing up the numbers. Then sew around the three folded sides of each pocket to secure, using a standard machine running stitch.

♥ When all 24 pockets are attached, fold over ½ in all around the main piece and iron to hold. Then fold over another ½ in on the two side and bottom edges. Sew around these three sides with the same stitch and colored thread used to hem the pocket tops.

♥ To make the channel at the top for hanging, fold over the top edge by ¾ in and sew across. Thread the dowelling through the channel, attach the ribbon to either end, and hang in position ready to fill with goodies for the days leading up to Christmas Eve. We used chocolate coins and chocolate tree decorations.

Wrapping
presents

IN BRITAIN ALONE, 8,000 tons of wrapping paper is used every year just on Christmas presents—the equivalent of 50,000 trees. It's un-ecological, uneconomical, and, in many cases, not even very attractive. Why buy into the wasteful gift-wrap industry when you can easily make or recycle your own? Get into the habit of keeping and recycling wrapping paper and save ribbons from clothes purchases or bunches of flowers as well as from other presents. Set aside a drawer or large box to store it in—the paper neatly folded and the ribbons carefully rolled—and keep scissors, scotch tape, silver pens, and other handy items there, too.

With the best will in the world, you will probably have to buy *some* paper. Tissue paper is cheap, recyclable, and easy to work with—and comes in jewel-bright colors. Layer two colors for an interesting mix, and choose a coordinating ribbon. Brown paper is a timeless classic, and easily smartened up with a band of contrasting-patterned paper from your recycled stash. Even black and white newspaper can look beautiful if teamed with bright red or silver ribbon, and is great for large, unwieldy gifts. Or go for a roll of white drawing paper, hand painting or potato printing designs of your choice (see page 28 for tips) or spelling the recipient's name in bright colors (children are great at this and can be cajoled or bribed into doing batches at a time). For small presents, use wallpaper samples, or photocopy textured fabric, such as a piece of crochet, on plain paper.

The key when saving on paper is to wrap the presents beautifully, as here. Place awkwardly shaped items in boxes first, and fold the paper carefully round the gift, using "hospital corners" as if making a bed (pulling the paper out straight from each end of the package and then folding in the edges diagonally to form a triangle). And let rip with the other adornments—use really good ribbon or glue on pompoms (see page 152) or lots of brightly colored shapes, sequins, or other decorative items from children's crafts kits. Layer one or two bands of ornate recycled paper around the present and tuck in a fresh or dried flower from the garden.

Many of the above ideas are illustrated opposite—for more on homemade cards see page 178.

Knitted
angel

THE ANGEL AT THE TOP is traditionally the finishing touch for any Christmas tree—the final task in the annual ritual of decorating the branches (see Felt decorations on page 215). And what could be prettier than this little knitted angel? She may look complicated but, in fact, is easy enough for anyone with a basic mastery of knit and purl stitches; the only relatively time-consuming part would be the shaping on the wings and head. A nice idea would be to make a few as Christmas presents for friends and family—then practice can make perfect! The pattern below can also be adapted to make little dolls for children; just leave out the wings and change the colors of the dress. The hair is simplicity itself as it is made from loops of running stitch with the wool not pulled tight. It goes without saying that small items such as this are great for using up any scraps or lengths of wool you might have left over from other creative projects.

You will need

- 4-ply wool in the following colors (use up ends to make this angel as it takes tiny amounts): ½ oz cream, tan or skin tone, pink, yellow, or something for hair
- Size 12 knitting needles
- Stuffing or cotton wool

Tension over stocking stitch

14 sts and 18 rows = 2 in

Abbreviations

See page 229

Arms (make 2)

Cast on 10 sts in cream, 2 sts in tan.

Work 6 rows in stocking st (knit one row, purl one row).

Cast off 12 sts.

The arms and legs naturally roll so that the reverse side of st st is on the outside. Catch together cast-on edge to cast-off edge in the direction that they have rolled. Sew in any loose ends.

Legs (make 2)

Cast on 12 sts in tan, 2 sts in pink or a contrast color.

Work 6 rows stocking st.

Cast off 14 sts.

Catch and sew edges as for the arms.

Body

Cast on 20 sts in cream.

Work 17 rows in st st.

Then knit 6 rows more.

Cast off.

Head

Cast on 4 sts in tan or skin tone.

ROW 1: Knit.

ROW 2: Purl.

ROW 3: Knit, inc 1 st at either end of row. (6 sts)

ROW 4: Purl.

Repeat rows 3 and 4 (8 sts).

Work 4 rows more in stocking st.

ROW 11: Knit, dec 1 st at either end or row. (6 sts)

ROW 12: Purl.

ROWS 13 & 14: As rows 10 and 11. (4 sts)

ROW 15: Purl.

ROW 16: Knit.

Cast off.

Wings (make 2)

Wings are all garter st (knit every row).

Cast on 6 sts in cream.

ROWS 1 & 2: Knit.

ROW 3: Knit, inc 1 st at either end of row. (10 sts)

ROW 4: Cast on 4 sts at beg of row, knit to end. (14 sts)

Work 3 rows in garter st.

ROWS 8-11: Rep last 4 rows. (18 sts)

ROW 12: Cast on 4 sts at beg of row, knit to end. (22 sts)

ROW 13: Knit, dec 1 st at beg of row.

ROW 14: Knit, dec 1 st at end of row.

ROW 15: Knit, dec 1 st at beg of row. (19 sts)

Cast off (this is the outside edge of your wing).

Skirt

Cast on 44 sts in cream and knit 2 rows.

ROW 3: Knit.

ROW 4: Purl.

ROWS 5-18: Rep rows 3 and 4, ending on a purl row.

ROW 19: K4, k2tog, * k3, k2tog, rep from * 6 times more, k3. (36 sts)

ROW 20: Purl.

ROW 21: K3, k2tog, * k2, k2tog, rep from * 6 times more, k3. (28 sts)

ROW 22: Purl.

ROW 20: K2, k2tog, * k1, k2tog, rep from * 6 times more, k3. (20 sts)

ROW 21: Purl.

Cast off.

Fold in half and sew the side seam of the skirt.

To make up

♥ For the head, sew side seams, then stuff from base. Embroider eyes with two small over stitches (see page 226) for each.

♥ To make hair, thread a darning needle with yellow yarn and stitch around the head with random running stitch (see page 226) but leaving loops instead of pulling the yarn flat.

♥ For the body, fold in half and catch the legs at each corner of the cast-on edge and sew across with running stitch, securing the legs in position as you sew. Sew the side seam of the body, then stuff the body and sew approximately 5 mm (¼ in) either side on cast-off edge for shoulders.

♥ Attach the base of the head to the "neck" space, using over stitch or a neat stitch as preferred.

♥ Place the skirt over the doll's body and use over stitch to catch the cast-off edge around the body approximately 1 cm (½ in) below the garter st detail of the body.

♥ Sew in any loose ends.

♥ To attach the wings, sew the cast-on edge of each wing to the center back of the angel's body.

Decorating for
Christmas

CLEARLY, EVERYONE HAS their own "look" or style when it comes to decorating the house for Christmas: the following sums up ours. Feel free to adapt or expand on these suggestions as you will, using whatever materials and treasured decorations you have at hand. What feels important is to simplify: fewer store-bought decorations means less expense and hassle. Making things from natural objects and materials found around the house and garden can become part of the life-enhancing rituals leading up to Christmas, especially if children are able to lend a hand. Freeing oneself from some of the commerciality of Christmas leaves room for the truly fundamental aspects of the festive period: acknowledging its spiritual significance in whatever way seems to chime with our beliefs and relishing time spent with friends and family.

Festive mantelpiece

There are all sorts of fancy Christmas decorations for sale in stores, but in our opinion, nothing can beat the traditional favorites, starting out with natural materials and adding lights and treasured items as you will. Build a roaring fragrant fire in the grate beneath and you are really ready for Father Christmas.

You will need

◆ Trailing ivy (can be pruned from garden)
◆ Sprigs of holly
◆ Pine cones, berries, and other woodland items, perhaps gathered on a winter' s walk
◆ Set of twinkle lights
◆ Baubles and other favorite decorations

To decorate the mantelpiece

♥ It is best to clear and dust your shelf or mantelpiece first, before draping the ivy in swags, anchoring them with the heavier sprigs of holly, and punctuating with pine cones, bright berries, and other natural objects.

♥ Weave a set of twinkle lights in among the foliage—plain white or red-hot chilli pepper lights look best for Christmas.

♥ Add a few baubles, other special decorations or cards as you see fit. It can be nice to give homemade cards some recognition by displaying them in a prominent place.

♥ A real fire in the grate is the true finishing touch. Stack plenty of wood alongside for a feeling of warmth and security, whatever the weather; maybe try to track down apple or pear wood, which burn with a gloriously atmospheric scent.

Felt decorations

Bursting with cheerful color and homespun charm, these felt decorations (see below and overleaf) couldn' t be simpler, and are a great way of involving children in pre-Christmas preparations. They could even make decorations to give as presents to friends, godparents, and teachers, slipped in with a homemade Christmas card. The selection of patterns overleaf is really just a guide—you can copy some, but also feel free to get creative with other Christmassy images, such as crowns, snowmen, and ivy leaves, as the mood takes you. Mix them with other traditional decorations on the tree or, if you prefer, show them off on their own on bare twiggy branches in a jug (in the spirit of the Easter tree on page 32), laid along the mantelpiece or strung up as a mobile.

How much time and effort you spend on each decoration is up to you. The quickest option is just to use running stitch (see page 225) around the edge, or you can decorate the felt with embroidery stitches as shown opposite. For instructions on embroidery stitches, see pages 225-6.

Add sequins (as for the Christmas tree opposite) or lightly stuff the felt shapes (with shredded old tights or tissue) to make three-dimensional decorations (as in the ivy and orange star). For the stockings, why not embroider names or short messages? A selection of these decorations could also be put in the pockets of the Advent calendar on page 202.

You will need

◆ Felt, which is generally much cheaper when sold by the yard than in smaller squares

◆ Ribbon (ideally recycled lengths from your ribbon stash, see page 206)

◆ Sewing threads in contrasting colors to felt

◆ Sequins (optional)

To make

♥ Using a paper pattern only where really necessary (but you may find the outlines given on page 241 helpful), cut out the decorations, using two layers of felt for each one. As with our heart (see page 215), you might choose to cut out some of the pieces of felt with pinking shears to add a pretty, deckled edging.

♥ Sew around the edge with tiny running stitches in a contrasting color to create a basic but attractive decoration, securing a loop of pretty ribbon as you sew, at the top edge with the running stitch.

♥ To make the decorations illustrated here, follow the instructions to the right. Or feel free to be led by your own creative urges.

Star, heart, and stocking

♥ These three lovely decorations are shown in the photograph on page 215. We used chain stitch to decorate the star, heart, and stocking (spelling "Noel" on the star, "PAX" on the heart, and for the hem edge of the stocking cuff).

♥ For the stocking, before sewing together the two main pieces, work a row of chain stitch across the bottom edge of the white cuff, attaching it to the stocking.

♥ Sew around the outside edge of the stocking with running stitch, but leave the top open, and attach the ribbon loop to the corner of the top back edge. Work a row of running stitches around the top of the stocking to secure the white cuff in place while allowing space for a chocolate or spiral sugar cane to be inserted into the stocking.

Bauble and holly leaf

♥ For the bauble, sew around the outside with running stitch, leaving a space about ¾ in wide to add stuffing. After stuffing, continue sewing up the gap with running stitch, adding the ribbon loop for hanging.

♥ For the holly (pictured right), sew the veins of the leaves with small back stitches, then sew two or three small circles of felt (for the berries) to the top near the ribbon.

Adding sequins

We sewed sequins to the bauble and Christmas tree. Using a continuous thread, add the sequins randomly all over the decoration, passing the thread between both pieces of felt to hide it. Or you could add the sequins before stitching the felt together.

Trimming the Christmas tree

Trimming the Christmas tree is a lovely ritual in which all the family can participate. Choose a time when you can work in an unhurried way—ideally towards the end of the afternoon or early evening so that the lights can be switched on with a degree of ceremony when it gets dark.

The idea of the "styled" tree, with all the objects newly bought to fit in with an agreed color scheme, is anathema to the Homemade approach. Instead, bring out vintage decorations that have become family heirlooms since your own childhood and beyond, plus newer ones made by hand, perhaps some of them by the children in your life. Homemade, handmade items bring an energy all of their own to the tree, adding to its significance as a family talisman, loaded with memories and associations, from year to year.

Like the eggs on the Easter tree (see page 32), your collection of tree decorations will become a treasured possession, which you can add to year by year. As well as handmade pieces, such as the embroidered felt shapes on the previous page, we also buy a few new or second-hand items every so often—from vintage finds on eBay to those picked up on trips around the country or travels abroad.

Less is most definitely less when it comes to tree decoration. In our book, you can' t have enough decorations and we load our trees with this eclectic mix of old and new until there is very little greenery showing in between.

We try to buy sustainable, non-dropping trees. Elspeth also has a smaller tree, bought for her daughter three years ago, which goes out into the garden in its pot after Twelfth Night, is kept well watered so the bushy new light green growth comes through each spring, and can be brought inside and decorated in the early days of December with miniature handmade paper chains and other treasured items.

When it comes to taking down the decorations on the traditional time of Twelfth Night (January 6 or Epiphany), make this a meaningful event, too. Put on the Christmas music for one last time, eat up those remaining mince pies and slices of Christmas cake, and savor the experience. Take time to wrap the decorations carefully, putting them away in mouse- and moth-proof containers, and look through your card collection one more time, saving any homemade ones that might provide inspiration for another year and cutting up other for Homemade tags next year. And give thanks in your heart for all the Christmases past and ones yet to come.

Handmade items bring an energy all of their own to the tree, adding to its significance as a family talisman, loaded with memories and associations, from year to year.

homemade basics

Homemade craft basics

Whether it's making cards, wrapping presents, labeling homemade produce, or dealing with little details, such as lining the Easter basket (see page 50) or fixing the patchwork fabric on the Denim chair (see page 68), having a well-stocked crafts kit ready can help everything go smoothly. Not having to hunt around the house to locate the right type of glue, roll of scotch tape, and so on will allow your creativity full rein, ensuring that your project will turn out the best it can possibly be.

Our own crafts kits are a combination of bought stuff—tried-and-tested glues, paints, and other products that we know will give a good performance—and goodies that we have saved from here and there, happy in the knowledge that they will be given another life in some creative project or other. We save everything, from pretty wrapping paper (larger areas only and with the creases ironed out where necessary) to rubber bands, ribbons from presents or bouquets of flowers—even the colored cotton tape from the heavy paper bags that are increasingly given away in clothes and other stores instead of plastic bags.

A large drawer can be handy for storing these items, with boxes or dividers within it to keep everything sorted. Also useful are mini chests of drawers made from wood or cardboard that can be stacked up next to or on top of one another and added to when required. Or you might prefer something more idiosyncratic to contain your kit, such as a sturdy reclaimed wicker laundry basket with old cookie tins housing all the bits inside, or a series of lovely old leather suitcases of varying sizes. The important thing is to have a system that works efficiently and looks pleasing into the bargain.

The *Homemade* craft kit

* Different types of glue for paper, fabric, and wood, and Superglue for fiddly items.
* Scotch tape and double-sided tape.
* Masking tape.
* Roll of brown parcel paper.
* Stick-on plain white labels of various sizes.
* Lead pencils.
* Colored crayons.
* Set of felt pens.
* Fountain pen and ink.
* Staple gun.
* Drawing pins.
* Tacks.
* Hammer.
* Paper (colored and white).

For wrapping presents

* Brown parcel paper.
* Newsprint and magazine paper.
* Tissue paper in a variety of colors.
* Rescued/reused wrapping paper sorted into larger pieces for reuse and smaller pieces for strips and borders (if you can find time to iron out creases, the paper will look much better).
* String.
* Raffia.
* Reels of new ribbon in one or two key colors. Red, for example, can perk up newsprint or brown paper and silver is good for use with tissue paper or even colored magazine pages.
* Silver paint, which is good for painting stars, names, and other adornments.
* Silver and gold pens.
* Pompoms and other embellishments that are easy to use and will perk up plainer wrapping.
* Old-fashioned brown paper luggage labels in various sizes or scraps of cardboard for making your own labels.

And for painting projects

* Primer/undercoat for dark and light colors.
* Outdoor and indoor eggshell paint: preferably water-based for ease of use and lower chemical content.
* White spirit: for cleaning brushes if using non-water-based paints.
* Brushes in various sizes, from 2–3 in wide for covering larger areas to pointed artist' s brushes for handpainting.
* Fabric paints and/or fabric crayons.
* Erasable pencil/chalk for marking out projects.

Sewing kit basics

It is good to have two sewing kits: one can be small and portable, containing the bare essentials (needles, thread, safety pins, and a spare button or two) that you keep in a handbag and use for mending on the go, and the other much more extensive— based at home and used for larger projects, such as those in this book. The following items are recommended for inclusion in the latter.

The *Homemade* sewing kit

✳ Basic sewing machine (not essential but certainly useful) and a variety of sewing machine needles.

✳ At least two pairs of sharp scissors: small, very sharp embroidery scissors (good for unpicking) and a good-quality pair of fabric shears. By including both pairs of scissors, you are ensuring that the fabric scissors will last a long time. Ideally, you would also include a medium pair of scissors for cutting paper patterns. Never using your sewing scissors for paper makes them stay sharp much longer.

✳ Pinking shears for making zigzag edges to hems (less likely to fray) and cutting fabrics such as felt in an attractive way. Their name comes from the common pink, in the genus *Dianthus*, or carnation, which has scalloped edges to its petals.

✳ Pins stuck in an attractive *Handmade* pincushion if possible (see page 170), though magnetic pin holders are also available. Many people find quilting pins with colored heads easier to handle, and they are certainly easier to see, making it less likely that you will leave pins in place on a finished item. The larger headed pins are particularly useful when working with knitting or crochet, as conventional pins get lost easily and can slip out of place in a loose open-weave structure.

✳ Hand-sewing needles in various sizes, including thicker darning needles for working with thicker thread or wool.

✳ Safety pins, fastened together for safety and convenience.

✳ Tailor's chalk for marking out patterns (this washes or brushes out easily).

✳ Cotton thread in various colors; a multi-colored skein is handy for a smaller kit, but more commonly used colors, such as black, white, and navy, are as well kept in longer reels.

✳ Tape measure that reads in imperial and metric. One that retracts inside a leather cover is useful and less likely to get damaged or lost.

✳ Poppers and hooks and eyes for fastening.

✳ Fusible fabric.

✳ Button box (see page 142) containing buttons of all shapes, colors, and sizes.

✳ Rag bag full of scraps and smaller pieces of fabric that you have saved up over the years.

✳ Steam iron for pressing fabric before, during and after making up.

Non-essentials, but useful

✳ Thimble, especially if you get sore fingers and thumbs.

✳ Seam ripper/unpicker.

✳ Ruler to provide a more solid edge than a tape measure.

✳ Embroidery threads in all colors.

✳ Tapestry wool for thicker embroidery and embellishments.

Where you keep your sewing equipment depends largely on the size of your kit and how much space is available in your home. Some people have an entire room of the house devoted to sewing and/or other crafts, with cupboards and drawers stuffed full of fabrics and colored thread. Others have just a small bag or box; perhaps a patchwork bag that has been specially made for the purpose, or a traditional box with hinged side sections that lift out. An ideal in-between option is a shelf or section of a cupboard, just for your sewing goodies.

What is important for motivational as well as practical reasons is that the kit should be well organized and attractively laid out. Make or buy handmade pin cushions and needle books for keeping sharp items safe; those made by children are often particularly charming. Save pretty old tins and jars for keeping other small items ordered.

Learning to sew

For more on courses and learning how to sew, see the Directory on page 243.

Basic stitches used in this book

Most of the instructions below and overleaf are based on those supplied on the Web site of the Embroiderer's Guild (www.embroiderersguild.com/stitch/stitches/). There are also some superb YouTube entries, some of which show the creation of the stitches very clearly, accompanied by music!

1 Back stitch

Bring the thread up through the fabric on the stitch line and then take a small backward stitch down through the fabric. Bring the needle through again a little in front of the first stitch, then take another backwards stitch, inserting the needle at the point where it first came through.

2 Blanket stitch

Push the needle up through the fabric a short way from the edge, hooking the rest of the thread around the top of the needle. Pull the needle through the fabric, keeping the lower thread out of the way so the thread forms a loop around the edge of the fabric. Repeat to create a line of linked stitches along the fabric edge.

3 Chain stitch

Having pulled the needle through the fabric, insert the needle next to where it emerged and bring the point out a short distance away. Pull the thread around the needle, keeping it under the needle's point, and pull the needle through the fabric to create a looped stitch. Holding down the loop, repeat to make a series of linked chains.

4 Cross stitch

Working on the canvas holes in groups of four, bring the needle up through the lower left hole (1) and take it down through the canvas one hole up and to the right (2). Bring it through to the front again one hole down (3) to form a half cross. Continue in this way to the end of the row, then complete the upper section of the cross. Cross stitch can be worked from left to right, as shown, or from right to left, but it is important that the upper half of each cross lies in one direction.

Cross-stitch fabric or Binca (used for making the Cross-stich no entry sign on page 184) comes in different "counts" (for example, "six count" means six holes per inch) and in a variety of colors. Start with a low-count fabric as your work will progress quicker and it is easier to use. You can buy it direct from www.threadsite.co.uk/tandem/fabrics/binca.html.

1 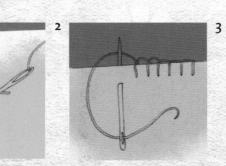 **2** 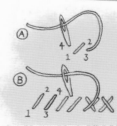 **3** 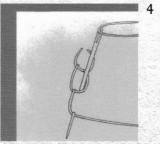 **4**

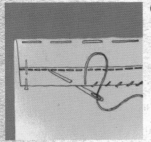
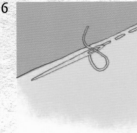
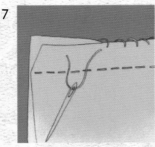
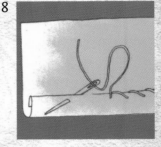

5 Hem stitch

Fold the hem horizontally with your thumb on the hem. Lay the end of your thread in the fold of the hem. Working from left to right, take a small back stitch through just the hem to anchor the thread. Moving a small way along the fabric to the right, pick up two threads from the work and pull gently. Then pick up two threads from the folded hem, to the right of the first stitch. Move on to the next two threads in the work, pull gently and then pick up two threads in the hem. Continue working in this way towards the corner.

6 Running stitch

Pass the needle in and out of the fabric, making sure that the surface stitches are of equal length. The stitches on the underside should also be of equal length, but half the size or less than the upper stitches.

7 Over stitch

This stitch is worked from the right side and is often used to join together pieces of fabric, or as an alternative to blanket stitch to prevent fraying. Place the pieces of work together with wrong sides facing, then bring the needle up through both layers from the underside. Repeat, always bringing the needle from the underside of the work. The thread binds together the two layers of fabric. Over stitch is especially useful for joining the fabric for a stuffed toy.

8 Slip stitch

A slip stitch can be used to repair a seam from the top. Push a threaded needle (be sure to knot the thread) through the material on one side of the opening, and then on the other. Continue until the seam is closed.

Making a buttonhole

These instructions tell you how to make a buttonhole using any sewing machine that can make a zigzag. If you have a newer machine, with fancy pre-programed buttonhole settings, you don't need to do it this way. Or you can handstitch by sewing around the open hole initially using over stitch and then buttonhole stitch, which is basically blanket stitch worked very closely together (see page 225). Neatly done, a hand-sewn buttonhole is a work of art. Most buttonholes are made with thread that matches the fabric color. Stick to that convention for any machine-sewn buttonholes, as no matter how well these are done they will be functional rather than decorative. For buttonholes beautiful enough to be a feature, hand-sewn or bound buttonholes are the answer.

✳ Mark out your buttonholes with tailor's chalk. They should be at least ¼ in larger than the buttons you intend to use. As a rule, buttonholes should be parallel with the edge of the garment so the button will pull on the end of the

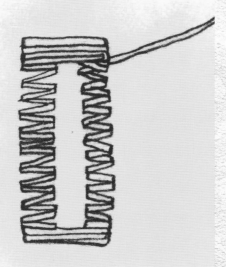

buttonhole, not the middle, where it would gap and look strange. The traditional marking is shaped like a capital "I," which emphasizes where the ends are so all of the buttonholes end up the same length.

✳ On the sewing machine, set your stitch width to maximum and your stitch length to o to create a wide zigzag that isn't going anywhere fast.

✳ Position the needle at the furthest end of the buttonhole marking. Stitch five or six zigzags to create the bar at that end of the buttonhole, finishing with your needle on the left. (Don't pull the fabric out or cut the thread after this stage— you want the thread to be taut between steps.)

✳ Set the stitch width to half of the maximum value and increase the stitch length a little. Stitch down the length of the buttonhole to the other end. Once again, don't pull the fabric out or cut the thread after this stage.

✳ Reset your stitch width to maximum and your stitch length to "o." Reposition the needle so its center position matches the center line of the buttonhole.

✳ Make five or seven zigzags at that end of the buttonhole. Be sure to do an odd number, so you end up with the needle at the extreme right. Leave the needle down and turn the entire garment around by 180 degrees.

✳ Once again, set the stitch width to half the maximum value and increase the stitch length a tiny bit. Position the needle so that its leftmost position matches the leftmost extent of the stitching just completed.

✳ Stitch down the length of the buttonhole back to where you started, being careful to stay parallel to the first side you sewed. Let the zigzag go a little into the starting zigzag for added strength.

✳ Using either buttonhole scissors, a seam unpicker, or ordinary sewing scissors, carefully cut open the buttonhole. Make sure you don't cut the stitching, particularly at the ends. Snip any loose threads and try passing the button through the hole.

Knitting basics

By far the best way to learn knitting is one-on-one from a more experienced friend or relative. But there are also many groups and walk-in "clinics" around, so for further information check out the Directory on page 245. The excellent Web site www.dominknitrix.com includes a gallery of pictures to help you learn various stitches, mattress stitch included.

The *Homemade* knitting kit

✳ A selection of knitting needles in different sizes: the ones in the book are size size 2 (Decorated coat hangers and iPod cover, see pages 36 and 136), size 3 (Fingerless gloves, see page 188), size 7 (Tea cosy, see page 138), and size 10½ (Woolly scarf, see page 186).
✳ Various crochet hooks of different sizes: handy for finishing off some of the knitting projects, such as the coat hanger and iPod covers (size 2mm and 2.5mm).
✳ Tape measure: ideally a retractable one in an attractive case.
✳ Small sharp scissors: embroidery scissors are ideal.
✳ Pencil and paper: for notes and making impromptu patterns.
✳ Stitch holder: at least one, for holding stitches when changing needles.
✳ Safety pins of various sizes.
✳ Needle gauge: for checking needle sizes.
✳ Circular needles: for making socks and gloves.
✳ Darning needles: for sewing flat pieces of knitting together.
✳ Button box (see page 142).
✳ Selection of small scraps of knitting yarn for embroidery and darning: these can be kept in a pretty tin or bag.

Most people keep knitting and crochet materials together as so many of the materials and pieces of equipment are duplicated, and crochet details are often used to finish off a knitting project. However, once a particular project is on the go, you may want to keep just the things pertaining to that item in the bag you keep with you at all times. It would help, therefore, to have separate knitting and crochet kits and include more than one of some of the items listed.

Knitting can be kept in anything from a large old cookie tin to a decorative bag made specially for the purpose, with different-sized pockets for needles, wool, and so on. Or how about storing your knitting and crochet needles in a fishing tackle box? The small compartments can be used for darning needles, quilting pins, safety pins, and any other bits of paraphernalia that you have. What you choose will depend partly on your own sense of style and partly on the size of your knitting projects—a crocheted blanket will take up more space than a pair of fingerless gloves, for instance.

Choosing yarn

Different yarns give different results: smooth and silky or rough and hairy. Long filaments create a different effect compared to short ones— compare the difference between an item made with a loose yarn, such as mohair, and one made with a tightly twisted yarns, such as mercerized cotton. So take all this into account when choosing yarn for a project.

Whatever yarn you choose, try to make it the best possible quality. After all the time and love you put into making something, you don' t want it to look tired and misshapen after only one wash.

Buying good knitting yarn now is a treat not a trauma. Gone are the days of scratchy wool and acrylic in nasty colors, and though the demise of the corner wool shop has been sad, the internet has made sourcing much easier in recent years. Numerous companies (see the Directory, pages 245–6) make beautiful ranges of pure and mixed yarn and have pure wool that washes well and feels soft and wearable.

The main problem is price: good yarn can be very expensive. Shop around for bargains, especially on the internet. There are hundreds of online yarn stores and, of course, eBay, all selling beautiful yarns at knockdown prices. Check out the brand first at your local wool shop or department store and then look it up online and see what you can find.

We have used mercerized cotton in this book for the coat hanger and iPod covers (see pages 36 and 136). This has a slight sheen to it, due to it being highly spun in manufacture. Ordinary 4-ply will make up the same pattern in the same way, but won't have the same luxurious look. When a pattern is using so little yarn, we think it is worth using mercerized instead of matt cotton to get the best possible effect.

Yarn usually comes in 2-oz balls but, for economy, try to find yarn on large hanks, or larger still, 1- lb 2-oz cones, which are a cheaper option when buying new.

Quite often yarn is reduced if it is an odd dye lot (see "Notes" right) and this is worth buying to add to your store when knitting or crocheting things that use small quantities, such as the Crochet squares (see page 180), Decorated coat hangers (see page 36), Fingerless gloves (see page 188), and Tea cosy (see page 138).

The make-do-and-mend mentality of the post-war generation meant it was common for people to unravel and re-knit their sweaters, steaming the wool to take out the kinks. While we wouldn't advocate this as essential, it certainly makes sense financially, provided you have time, the next time your child outgrows a nice hand-knit or you see an item made from a lovely yarn but don't like the style.

Notes for knitters

✳ ALWAYS work a tension swatch, no matter how little time you have. Then check it against the pattern and change your needles accordingly if necessary.
✳ The knitting and crochet tensions quoted on all the patterns in this book are a guide only. Every knitter has a personal tension— whether tight or loose.

✳ To check your tension, knit a square to the size given in the pattern and using the stitch from the pattern. When the square is complete, lay it on a flat surface and, using a tape measure, count the number of stitches and then the number of rows.
✳ If you have more stitches or rows than the tension indicated, use slightly smaller needles. If you have fewer stitches or rows, try using larger needles.
✳ The above also means that some knitters may use more or less yarn than that quoted.
✳ If buying more than one ball of the same-colored yarn, make sure they all have the same batch number—this is printed on the ball band. Although they may look the same to the naked eye, the same color from different dye batches will always show on the finished piece and spoil the uniform effect.
✳ When it's time to put your knitting away, pop a cork on the end of needles to stop the stitches falling off.
✳ Never leave your knitting in the middle of a row or there may be an obviously larger stitch in the middle once it is finished.

Abbreviations used for the Homemade projects
cont continue
col color
dec decrease/decreasing
inc increase/increasing
k knit
MC main color
p purl
rep repeat
RS right side
st/sts stitches
tog together

Crochet basics

In Victorian times up until the mid 20th century, crochet was used extensively for making and decorating clothes and household items. Children were taught to knit and crochet at school, but, like knitting, it fell out of fashion and the skill has been more widely lost in recent years. The huge resurgence in knitting, however, has led to crochet becoming another skill that people interested in handicrafts are keen to learn.

Crochet is as simple as knitting, some find it is easier. Ros learned to crochet before she could knit (she was only seven), and her first project was a doll's blanket. Just as with knitting, there are lots of different crochet stitches that can vary the look and texture of your work. Some styles are easier to achieve with crochet than with knitting; for instance, the undulating pattern of the crochet coat hanger cover on page 38 would be much harder to achieve if knitted.

Just Google "how to crochet" and you'll find thousands of Web sites packed with advice and able to teach you everything you need to get started. Because crochet used to be so popular, there are lots of amazing vintage patterns about—good sources include www.annalaia.com/ or www.knitting-crochet.com/crochet/antiquecrochet.html. Alternatively, try eBay or your local thrift shop; the latter will probably have a box of old patterns—anyone for a crochet bikini?

One of the oddest patterns Ros came across has to be one for crochet sleeves for your piano legs. She also has a pattern for a pair of crochet indoor sandals and recently saw a pattern for a baby's bottle cover. Vintage patterns that could easily become stylish, trendy, and covetable include the many for crochet flowers and jewelry.

The *Homemade* crochet kit

✳ A selection of crochet hooks of different sizes. The ones used in this book are 2mm and 2.5mm (the coat hanger and iPod covers, see pages 38 and 136).
✳ Tape measure: ideally a retractable one in an attractive case.
✳ Small sharp scissors: embroidery scissors are ideal.
✳ Pencil and paper: for notes and making impromptu patterns.
✳ Stitch holder: at least one—for holding stitches when changing hooks.
✳ Safety pins of various sizes.
✳ Darning needles: for sewing together flat pieces of crochet.
✳ Button box (see page 142).
✳ Selection of small scraps of knitting yarn for embroidery or darning: these can be kept in a pretty tin or bag within the bag.

Most items for crochet tend to be smaller than those for knitting—and the hooks are smaller than needles for a start—so the chances are that your crochet kit will fit into a smaller box, bag, or tin than the *Homemade* knitting kit listed on page 228. Whether you choose a zip-up or closed-hinge receptacle rather than an open one depends largely on whether you will be taking your kit out with you (on the bus or train or even to the cinema), or keeping it at home, and whether you need to keep your work and yarn protected from the ravages of children and/or pets. Choose something attractive, though, which will help you keep your work in order and make you want to pick it up often.

Choosing yarn

Traditionally, crochet yarn is a fine cotton, tightly twisted to avoid splitting. It gives a firmer finish to your work than other yarns, which was important for household objects that were commonly crocheted from mid 1800 to around 1950, and are still produced today by artisans in some European and south American countries. The yarn is still available and is usually referred to as crochet cotton. This fine cotton is best suited to lace work and—unless you are working from a vintage pattern, making something like traditional table linens (hardly likely if you are a beginner)—is far too fine for contemporary patterns and styles. Although you may be making small crochet flowers in the traditional manner, working from a contemporary color palette would make them into incredibly fashionable accessories.

Ros tends to use knitting yarns in all her crochet work as the patterns require thicker yarns. It is vital that the yarn you choose is appropriate for the design and that you avoid anything knobbly or with a slub, as these cause problems when working stitches together, common in crochet patterns.

See also Knitting basics (pages 228–9).

Notes for crocheters

See also Knitting basics (pages 228–9).

Abbreviations used in the Homemade ideas

ch chain
dc double crochet
sl st slip stitch
sp space
tr treble

Hook sizes

Crochet hooks are made from aluminum, plastic, bamboo, or sometimes bone.

Steel hooks	Aluminum hooks
14	B-1
13	C-2
12	D-3
11	E-4
10	F-5
9	G-6
8	7
7	H-8
6	I-9
5	J-10
4	K-101/2
3	L-11
2	M/N-13
1	N/P-15
0	P/Q
00	Q
	S

Cooking basics

Cooking with the right equipment is almost as important as using the right ingredients. Apart from a bustling sense of efficiency that really helps everything along, a good cooking kit can add immeasurably to the pleasures of the task in hand. A heavy glass bowl, possibly with a lip for pouring, in which to whisk eggs; the correct-size baking pans and cookie sheets; a pretty cooling rack and fun, well-made cookie cutters can all contribute to good cake-making, while unusual jars and bottles and good labels and pens are essential for finishing jams and chutneys in style.

The *Homemade* baking kit

✳ Mixing bowls: for mixing cake ingredients and incorporating the air that helps them rise. A set of nesting ones may be an attractive and useful option.
✳ Wooden spoons for mixing.
✳ Large metal spoons for folding in flour.
✳ Rubber spatulas for scraping bowls clean.
✳ Baking pans for cakes and cookie sheets for shortcakes and cookies (see right).
✳ Wire balloon whisk for beating air into eggs and/or an electric hand whisk (the purists swear by the former, but the latter makes life easier and quicker).
✳ Wire cooling racks for allowing air to circulate all around cakes when they come out of the oven. If stood on a flat surface, the bases can go soggy.
✳ Glass measuring jug: for measuring liquid ingredients at a glance.
✳ Rolling pin: an old-fashioned wooden (or even marble) rolling pin is indispensable for rolling out the marzipan for our Simnel cake (see page 58), not to mention pastry.
✳ Plain and fluted cutters: for small cakes, cookies and shortcakes. Never twist the cutter as you cut—just press down once and remove. Twisting can make for very strange shapes.
✳ Palette knife: useful for loosening cakes, including lifting cup cakes from baking pans and scones from baking trays.
✳ Nylon piping bag with one or two plain or starred nozzles for cake decorations—or buy ready-made icing in nozzle tubes.

✳ Wire or plastic sieves: for sifting the likes of flour and confectioner' s sugar to remove lumps and allow air in.
✳ Good scales are essential for baking and jam making. Proper balance scales may be expensive, but they do last a lifetime; cheap, flimsy spring scales with needle indicators will not, and often work out more expensive in the long run.

Tips for good cake making

✳ Get out all your ingredients before you start. Not only do you know for sure that you have them all; it will also make you feel calmer and more organized—a feeling that only contributes to good cooking. Most importantly, this practice should also bring all the ingredients to room temperature before you start.
✳ Preheat the oven so it is at the required temperature before you put the filled baking pan in to bake.
✳ Use good-quality baking pans of the right size for the recipe (see below).
✳ Cool thoroughly on a wire rack.

Baking pans

It is important to use good baking pans, and to use the correct size—even half an inch difference in diameter can upset the cooking times and the overall appearance and texture of the cake. The tins specified in this book are a standard size, cupcake tins and cookie sheets that can be found in any reasonably stocked kitchen shop or department store. Quality is important, as the heavier they are, the less likely they are to burn—plus they last longer. The depth is especially important for sponge tins, as without any depth above it, the cake won' t rise: use a sponge tin that is at least 4 cm (1½ in) deep. Many people complain about flat sponges when it wasn' t the recipe that was the problem; it was that the sponge had nowhere to go.

Non-stick tins are definitely easiest to use, though one is never too sure of all those chemicals used in the manufacturing process, and they can let you down sometimes. Non-stick springform tins—hinged so that the cake simply pops free when done—are the best by far. Once you have used one, you will never go back to the old-fashioned sort. Always grease and line any baking pan, non-stick or otherwise, just to be sure that the finished cake comes away easily, without getting stuck and/or broken in the process.

Lining and greasing a round tin

✳ Grease the baking pan with the same sort of fat as is used in the recipe, smearing it evenly all over the inside of the pan and into any corners, if there are any. Keep folded-up butter papers in the fridge door for this purpose, smearing more butter on if necessary.

✳ Cut a strip of parchment paper slightly longer than the circumference of the pan and 3 in higher than its depth. Fold the paper back about 1 in along its length, then snip it at an angle at intervals up to the fold.

✳ Press the paper around the sides of the pan so the snipped edge overlaps the base of the pan for a snug fit.

✳ Cut out a circle of parchment paper—using the pan as a template—to fit over the snipped paper over the base. Grease again lightly with fat. For extra crispness on the outside of the cake, sprinkle the pan with flour.

Care of baking pans

Some people never wash their baking pans, simply wiping them to avoid rust. The best way to take care of them, however, is to wash in hot water and dry well immediately afterwards, on a making sure all the moisture has been banished before storing away in a cupboard.

Storing cakes

There is nothing nicer than a row of pretty, well-stocked baking pans in your larder or ranged along your kitchen shelf. They are preferable to plastic boxes for practical as well as aesthetic reasons as metal is non-porous and cannot harbor smells and bacteria in the way that plastic can, however carefully you wash it.

Be careful if you are tempted by old pans in thrift shops, however, as they often have rust on them, which can contaminate the cakes and smell.

Also do not be tempted to store cakes and cookies in the same pan, as the moisture from the cakes will make the cookies soggy. For short-term storage, wrap cakes in aluminum foil, but if you' re storing a rich fruit cake, such as the Simnel cake on page 58, for a longer period, then use a double layer of greaseproof paper on the inside and foil on the outside—the acid in the fruit can corrode the foil if it comes into direct contact with it and cause mold.

Sterilizing jars and bottles

Sterilized jars and bottles are absolutely crucial for storing jams, jellies, sloe gin, and elderflower cordial if they are not to be at risk from going mouldy. The traditional method for sterilizing involves scrubbing the jars well in warm soapy water, rinsing in clean water, and placing them to dry in a cool oven (275°F). But glass that is hot and clean from a dishwasher is pretty much sterile, and this is a lot less demanding—even if you have to time the cycle to be ready when you need the jars, as it is important that they should be filled when hot.

Alternatively, sterilize the jars and bottles in a microwave by filling each jar a quarter full with water and microwaving on high for 10 minutes—again, use while warm.

Jam will benefit from circles of greaseproof paper being placed over the surface of the jam—this further prevents contamination, but be sure to wash your hands scrupulously first.

Jam-making tips

✳ Always use a stainless steel pan rather than an aluminum one as aluminum may react with the acid in the fruit. Buy as large a pan as possible as, when the mixture comes to the "rolling boil" required for setting, it will rise way up the sides of the pan.

✳ A good heavy bottom to the pan will also help prevent burning.

Gardening basics

If you have a large garden or go the whole hog and take on an allotment, you will no doubt have a shed full of gardening paraphernalia. But for those who are just starting out, and fancy a foray into some of the simpler gardening projects outlined in this book, such as the Easter basket (see page 50) or recycled containers (see page 84), here are a few suggestions. The information on sowing seeds (see page 44) contains all you need for getting your own seedlings started.

The *Homemade* gardening kit

* Hand trowel: for digging holes and spooning out soil.
* Hand fork: for weeding and dividing larger plants into smaller ones for filling containers, such as violas for the Easter basket and the Summer salad trough (see page 110).
* Secateurs: for removing any dead or dying material.
* Scissors: for above, plus snipping string and any labeling needs.
* Hammer and nails: for repairing reclaimed containers and knocking holes in the base of recycled containers.
* Electric drill: for making holes in more resistant containers.
* Garden wire and twine: for tying up plants and guiding plants to supports or trellis.
* Larger tubs or washtubs: for placing under plants being potted, so as not to mess up the whole space.

Tips for re-potting

* Make sure all of your desired containers have sufficient drainage holes and create more if necessary (banging nails on to a block of wood held as a buffer inside the bucket helps).
* Get all of your plants out and give them a good soak with water prior to planting.
* Line very holey containers, such as baskets or rusty buckets, with plastic by stapling into place with a staple gun.
* Place large chips of broken pot over the holes in the base of the container to ensure the escape route for excess water is not blocked, but at the same time not too free-draining.

* Add a minimum 2-in layer of pebbles or gravel to the base to help anchor the plant and reduce your soil needs. Lightweight granules can be found for roof terraces or other areas where excess weight, particularly when the plants are wet, might be a problem.
* Sprinkle in a little soil mixed with compost around the base, along with a handful of slow-release fertilizer, such as blood, fish, and bone.
* Plant the largest plants, such as trees or shrubs, first, digging a hole at least as large again as the original container and firming down new soil around the roots.
* Arrange all the other smaller plants—still in their nursery containers or, if dug up from the garden, in clumps of soil—on the soil around the larger plant. Adjust them according to height and color, standing back to take stock on several occasions.
* When the desired effect has been achieved, gently knock the plants out of their pots, dig appropriately sized holes in your chosen positions, and pop the plants in place, filling in around them with soil mixed with compost. Pat the soil down gently with your hands around the base of the stem of each plant and water well.
* Keep an eye on young plants in their first few weeks outside, particularly if the weather is dry. Give them a good soaking every few days (this is better for root development than watering every day).
* If, at any point, the roots of a plant protrude excessively through the holes in the base of the pot, that means the plant has outgrown the container and needs potting-on once. Simply repeat the process described above.
* For some ideas for recycled containers, see pages 84–9.

Patterns

The patterns we have used are very simple and, in most cases, consist of a hard outline with a dotted line if there is a seam allowance or a line of stitching. Follow the instructions for how many pieces to cut and where material needs to be doubled and/or placed on a fold. In some instances there are other markings that need to be transferred such as seam allowances and button and buttonhole positions.

Provided the pattern does not need sizing up, trace the outline plus any other detailing on to tracing paper. Pin the paper on to the fabric, as instructed, and cut around the fabric— also cutting through the paper, if this is the first time you have used the pattern. Using pinking shears can help prevent fraying on straight edges. Transfer any extra markings to the fabric

using dressmaker' s chalk—check that it comes out of the fabric easily. In the case of button positions or a seam allowance, you may prefer to place a pin in the correct place for reference, making sure the place where the pin disappears beneath the fabric to come up again is at the precise position that you want to record. You could also use a water-soluble pen or a tailor' s tack. The latter is illustrated on the Web site http://sewing.about.com/library/sewnews/library/aamarking04 04a.htm. By far the easiest way to scale up the patterns (such as the Child' s summer dress on page 238) is to use a photocopier, enlarging by the percentage increase indicated on the pattern.

Egg cosies

See project on page 20
Enlarge pattern to 150 percent to get to actual size required

Flower

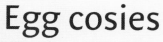

Chicken
cut 2

Wing
cut 2

Simple
egg cosy
cut 3

Lavender cats

See project on page 62
Enlarge pattern to 140 percent to
get to actual size required

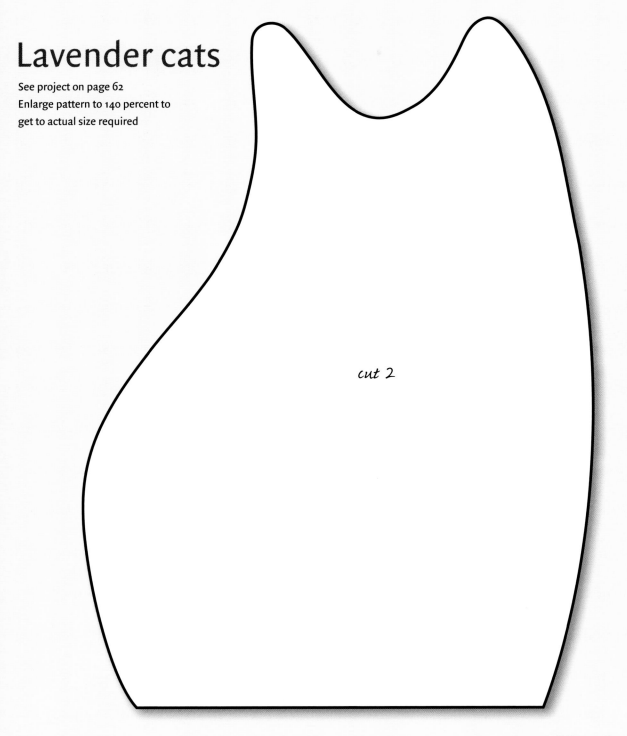

cut 2

Child's summer dress

See project on page 70
Enlarge pattern to 265% to get to
actual size required

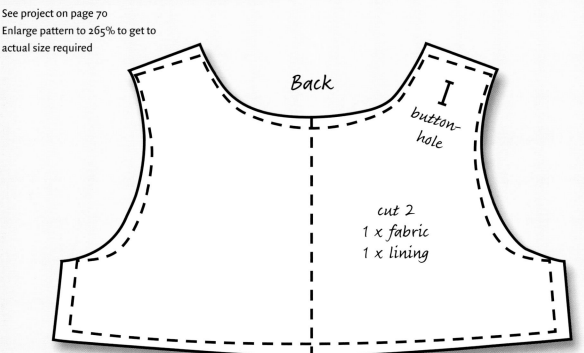

Back

I
button-
hole

cut 2
1 x fabric
1 x lining

Inner dotted line for age 1   Outer solid line for age 3

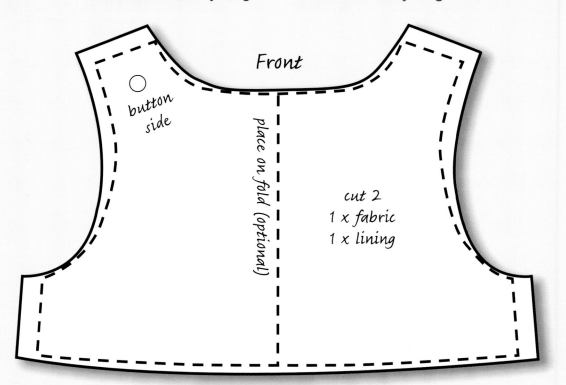

Front

button
side

place on fold (optional)

cut 2
1 x fabric
1 x lining

Skirt

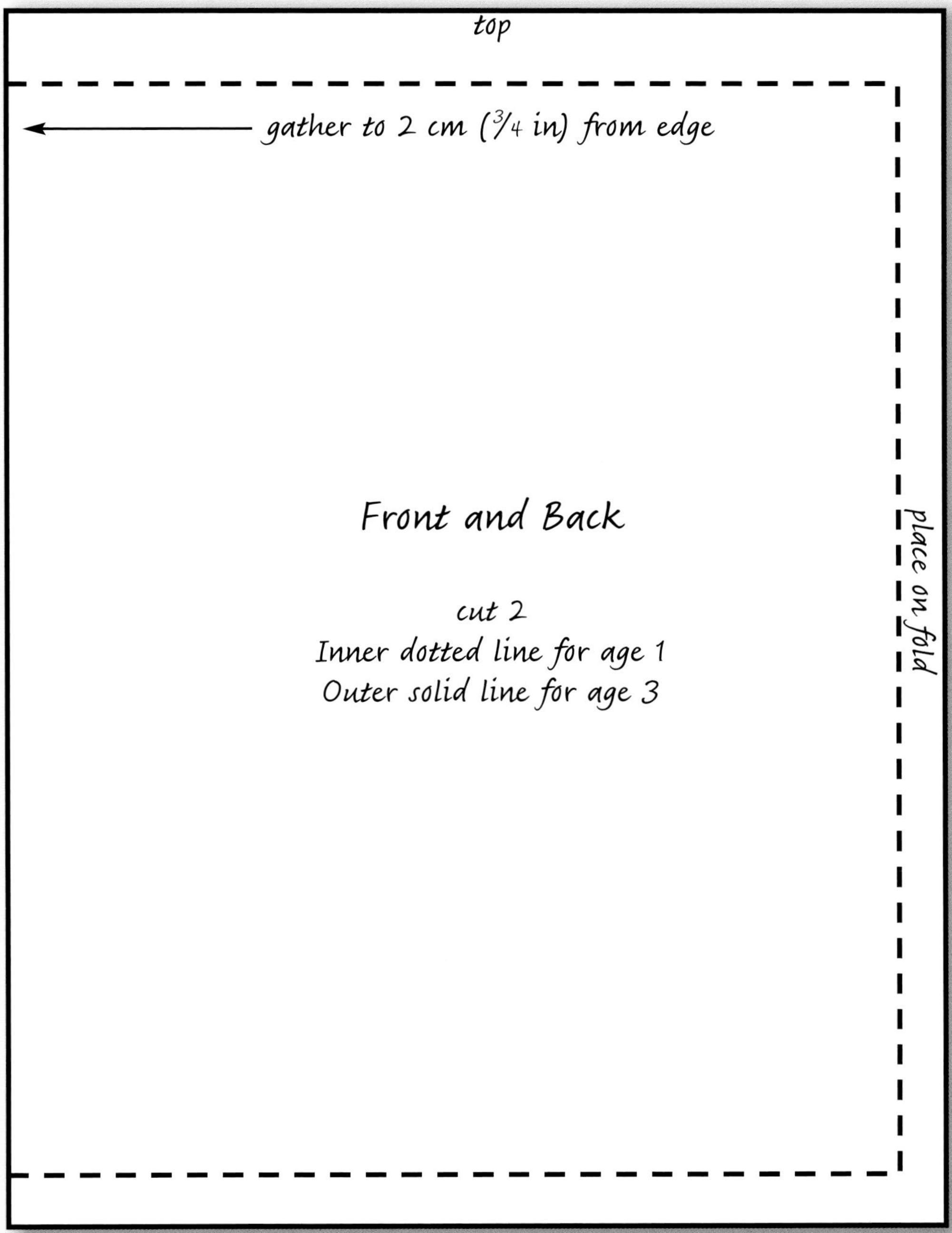

top

gather to 2 cm (³⁄₄ in) from edge

Front and Back

cut 2
Inner dotted line for age 1
Outer solid line for age 3

place on fold

Side straps   cut 2

place on fold

Age 1

Age 3

Tea cosy and Beach bag

See projects on pages 138 (Tea cosy) and 100 (Beach bag)

Illustrations are drawn actual size

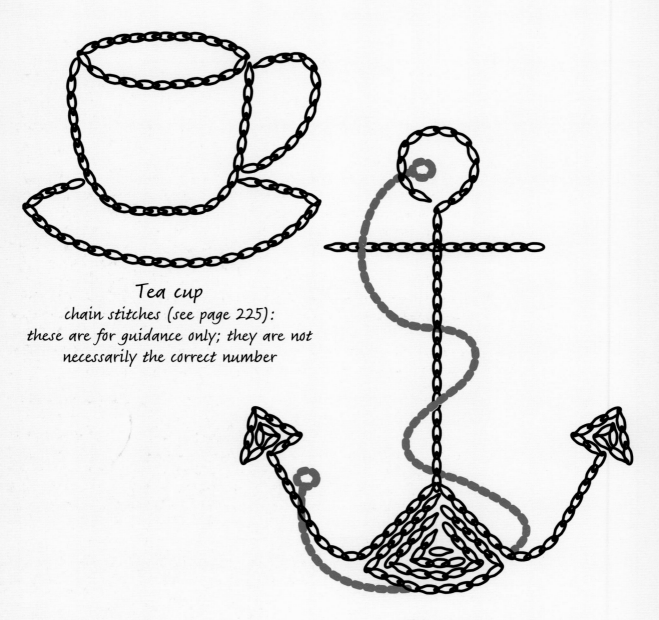

Tea cup
chain stitches (see page 225):
these are for guidance only; they are not
necessarily the correct number

Anchor
chain stitches (see page 225): these are for guidance
only; they are not necessarily the correct number.
Blue is rope ribbon wrapped around anchor

Christmas decorations

See project on page 216

Enlarge patterns to 143% to get to actual size required

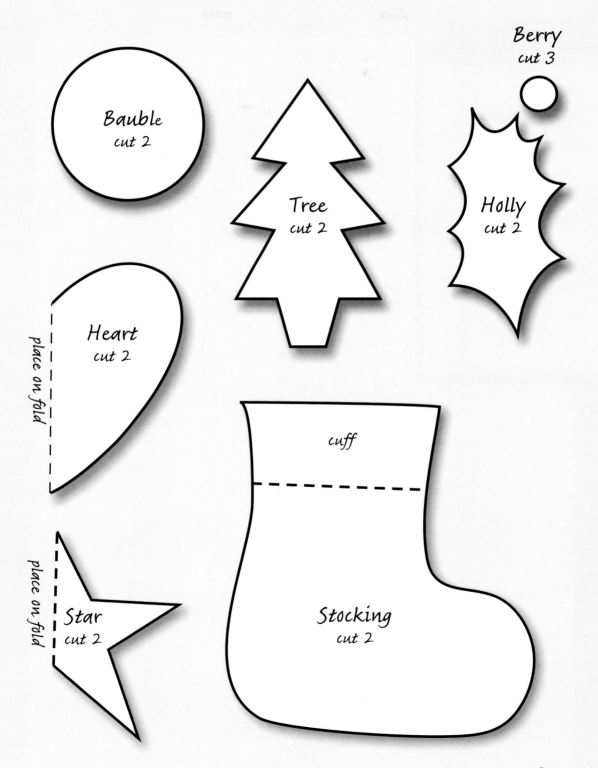

Bauble
cut 2

Tree
cut 2

Berry
cut 3

Holly
cut 2

Heart
cut 2

place on fold

cuff

Star
cut 2

place on fold

Stocking
cut 2

Index

Acknowledgments

Firstly we would both like to thank Benjamin J. Murphy for his perfectionist's eye and dedication—his photographs have made this book truly beautiful. Also Mary Mathieson for her wonderful illustrations, and for contributing so much to various projects throughout the book.

Huge thanks are also due to Jane Turnbull, our brilliant agent, who championed this idea from the start; Denise Bates and all at HarperCollins who took it up and ran with it and really went the extra measure to produce such a beautiful book; Andrew Barron for the elegant design; Emma Callery for her skillful editing, and Charlotte Allen for all her hard work on publicity. We would also like to thank Piers Feltham and Chiara Menage, Christopher Matthews and Phillipa George, and Caddy and Chris Wilmot-Sitwell for allowing us to take photographs in their gardens.

Many other people have helped inspire our own creativity and have contributed to this book in so many different ways. They include Vanessa Aitchison, Michael Badger, Jane Brocket, Carolyn Brookes-Davies, Karen Jensen-Jones, Carol Lloyd Waters, Karen Long, Gary Kaye, Monica McMillan, Lawrence Morton, Charlene Mullen, Kristin Perers, Francine Raymond, Maureen and Phil Rooksby, Jo Self, and not forgetting craft club members especially Lorraine Sorrel, Caddy Wilmot-Sitwell, Kim West, Rebecca Tanqueray, and Tessa Brown and "knitting ladies" Katy Jaffey, Grace Hodge, Vicky Cryer, and Sarah Bratby.

Thank you all!
Ros: I would also like to thank my mum, Ruth Badger, for teaching me to sew when I was very young, and her sister Joan Kenwright who, along with my mum, spent hours "on the sewing machine" throughout my childhood; also my grandmother Mary Elizabeth Hunter for teaching me how to crochet when I was seven years old.

Elspeth: I would also like to thank my mother and father, Margaret and Alec Thompson, for bringing me up in a home where making things was second nature, and my sisters Rebecca Edwards and Sarah Hanshaw, whose homes are filled with beautiful things they have made over many years. Thank you for all you have taught me and for the inspiration and encouragement.

Notes

ALSO AVAILABLE

Spinning, Dyeing & Weaving: Self-Sufficiency
by Penny Walsh

This handbook looks at where different fibers come from, how to grow and harvest them, and how to prepare them for spinning. It also includes the principles of spinning as well as information on how to dye your fibers with natural dyestuff.
$12.95 Hardcover • 128 pages

Keeping Chickens: Self-Sufficiency
by Mike Hatcher

Packed full of information on basic housing costs and requirements, food and water requirements, disease prevention, and breeding, this book also includes a comprehensive section on the breeds available and a list of resources.
$12.95 Hardcover • 128 pages

Home Brewing: Self-Sufficiency
by John Parkes

This new handbook includes everything you'll need to brew a variety of beers at home, from equipment and techniques to inside secrets from a professional brewer. John Parkes, an experienced brewmaster, explains how anyone can produce delicious beer with the help of just some basic equipment and a few key skills.
$12.95 Hardcover • 128 pages

Household Cleaning: Self-Sufficiency
by Rachelle Strauss

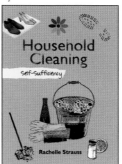

Most conventional store-bought cleaning products are packed full of chemicals, many of which are harmful to the environment and your health. You'll be pleasantly surprised to discover that your kitchen cupboard already stocks the alternative supplies you'll need to transform your home into a clean, safe, and fresh-smelling haven!
$12.95 Hardcover • 128 pages

Beekeeping: Self-Sufficiency
by Joanna Ryde

While beekeeping is about managing, controlling, and understanding the honey bee, there is also the pleasure found in harvesting and eating your own honey! All aspects of beekeeping are explained inside this essential guide: the basic tools and equipment needed, detailed advice on when to harvest honey, and the many tasty things you can make.
$12.95 Hardcover • 128 pages

Preserving: Self-Sufficiency
by Carol Wilson

All you need is a heavy-based pan, a funnel, a sugar thermometer, and glass storage jars. Ingredients, popular fruits and vegetables, sugars, cooking techniques, storage information, helpful hints and tips, and 60 delicious recipes make this book your one-stop guide to successful preserving.
$12.95 Hardcover • 128 pages

Cheese Making: Self-Sufficiency
by Rita Ash

The information here covers every aspect of cheese making at home, including the tools and equipment needed, and basic recipes and advice on setting up a small cheese-making business. Rita Ash shows just how simple it is to make cheese, and how, with a little bit of care and attention, anyone can produce delicious cheeses at home.
$12.95 Hardcover • 128 pages

ALSO AVAILABLE

Homesteading: A Back to Basics Guide to Growing Your Own Food, Canning, Keeping Chickens, Generating Your Own Energy, Crafting, Herbal Medicine, and More
Edited by Abigail R. Gehring

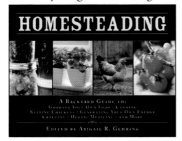

From what to eat to supporting sustainable restaurants to avoiding dry cleaning, this book offers information on anything a homesteader needs—and more.
$24.95 Hardcover • 464 pages

Self-Sufficiency: A Complete Guide to Baking, Carpentry, Crafts, Organic Gardening, Preserving Your Harvest, Raising Animals, and More
Edited by Abigail R. Gehring

Whether the goal is to live entirely off the grid or just to shrink their carbon footprints, families will find this book a thorough resource and a great inspiration.
$24.95 Hardcover • 464 pages

Back to Basics: A Complete Guide to Traditional Skills, Third Edition
Edited by Abigail R. Gehring

The hundreds of projects, photographs, charts, and illustrations in *Back to Basics* will help you graft trees, raise chickens, craft a hutch table with hand tools, make blueberry peach jam, and more!
$24.95 Hardcover • 464 pages

Simpler Living: A Back to Basics Guide to: Cleaning, Decorating, Storing, Decluttering, Streamlining, Organizing, and More
by Jeff Davidson, Foreword by Mark Victor Hansen

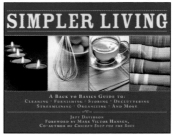

Filled with tips on how to uncomplicate your routine, eliminate stress at home and work, and more, this book will help you find time to do the things you love.
$24.95 Hardcover • 452 pages

The Ultimate Book of Decorative Knots
by Lindsey Philpott

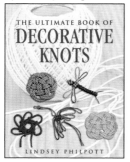

In this handsomely illustrated full-color volume, renowned knot expert Lindsey Philpott shows you how to tie symmetrical and attractive knots, both simple and intricate, that can be used for a wide variety of practical and ornamental purposes.
$29.95 Hardcover • 640 pages

The Illustrated Hassle-Free Make Your Own Clothes Book
by Joan Wiener Bordow and Sharon Rosenberg

Readers will embrace the step-by-step illustrations, clear and encouraging prose, and timeless collection of clothes in this book, which promises to be both an indispensable resource and a much-noticed collectible on every hipster's bookshelf.
$14.95 Paperback • 160 pages

The Encyclopedia of Monograms: Over 11,000 Motifs for Designers, Artists, and Crafters
by Leonard G. Lee

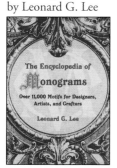

The remarkable *Encyclopedia of Monograms*—filled with over 11,000 handsomely engraved initials, ciphers, crests, insignias, emblems, badges, and shields—is a resource of fantastic scope that will be useful to anyone working in the field of graphic design.
$14.95 Paperback • 368 pages

Swedish Knits: Classic and Modern Designs in the Scandinavian Tradition
by Paula Hammerskog & Eva Wincent

Swedish designs have inspired modern knitting in how yarn is used, what designs are handsome, and also what is functional. This book brings the long-standing Swedish tradition up-to-date with pieces that are as hip as they are fun to make.
$27.95 Hardcover • 192 pages